PUSHING THE AGENDA

Today's presidents enter office having campaigned on an ambitious policy agenda, eager to see it enacted, and willing to push so that it is. The central question of presidents' legislative leadership, therefore, is not a question of resolve but a question of strategy: By what means can presidents build winning coalitions for their agenda? *Pushing the Agenda* uncovers the answer. It reveals the systematic strategies presidents employ to influence Congress and the conditions that determine when those strategies work – or don't. Drawing on an eclectic array of original evidence – spanning presidents from Dwight Eisenhower to George W. Bush – Matthew N. Beckmann finds that modern presidents' influence in Congress is real, often substantial, and, to date, largely underestimated.

Matthew N. Beckmann is Assistant Professor of political science at the University of California, Irvine, where he studies Washington politics, particularly those involving the White House. His work has appeared in the *Journal of Politics*, the *Journal of Theoretical Politics*, *Political Research Quarterly*, and *Political Communication*. Professor Beckmann received his BA from the University of California, Los Angeles, and his PhD from the University of Michigan.

"A critical part of the new generation of presidency research, Matthew Beckmann's *Pushing the Agenda* takes complex formal and informal theories seriously and then asks, 'is this really how presidential influence works?' His distinction between endgame, where votes matter most, and 'earlygame,' where cooperation over agendas matters most, constitutes an original theoretic as well as empirical contribution that academics in every setting will begin to take up in their own research. His analysis of presidential 'influence' within these two contexts breathes new life into a traditional concept rendered moribund by two decades of identification with measures of 'voting success' by demonstrating that when agendas matter and when votes matter, presidents matter and not at the margins either, but at the core. This book represents a foundation on which to construct a new generation of understanding and relevancy for presidency research."

> – Terry Sullivan, Hoover Institution, Stanford University,
> and University of North Carolina at Chapel Hill

"Matthew Beckmann's *Pushing the Agenda: Presidential Leadership in U.S. Lawmaking, 1953–2004*, is a major contribution to our knowledge about presidential legislative power. He uses rich and innovative quantitative and qualitative analysis of the last half-century's presidential-congressional interactions to explain presidential power on the Hill. His well-written and unique analysis focuses on presidential strategies and successes and failures of presidential influence in Congress. It is a must-read for anyone interested in the presidency and Congress."

> – James A. Thurber, American University

Pushing the Agenda

Presidential Leadership in U.S. Lawmaking, 1953–2004

Matthew N. Beckmann

University of California, Irvine

CAMBRIDGE
UNIVERSITY PRESS

CAMBRIDGE UNIVERSITY PRESS
Cambridge, New York, Melbourne, Madrid, Cape Town, Singapore,
São Paulo, Delhi, Dubai, Tokyo

Cambridge University Press
32 Avenue of the Americas, New York, NY 10013-2473, USA

www.cambridge.org
Information on this title: www.cambridge.org/9780521162913

First published 2010

Printed in the United States of America

A catalog record for this publication is available from the British Library.

Library of Congress Cataloging in Publication Data

Beckmann, Matthew N., 1975–
Pushing the agenda : presidential leadership in U.S. lawmaking,
1953–2004 / Matthew N. Beckmann.
    p.   cm.
Includes bibliographical references and index.
ISBN 978-0-521-76014-0 (hardback) – ISBN 978-0-521-16291-3 (paperback)
1. Presidents–United States.   2. Political leadership–United
States.   3. Legislation–United States.   4. Executive power–United States.
5. United States–Politics and government–1945–1989.
6. United States–Politics and government–1989– I. Title.

JK516.B39   2010
352.23′6097309045 – dc22   2009038064

ISBN 978-0-521-76014-0 Hardback
ISBN 978-0-521-16291-3 Paperback

Contents

Dedicated to my parents, Bob and Mary Lou

Figures

Tables

Acknowledgments

As it turns out, writing the acknowledgments is the hardest part: too many debts, too few words, and probably not the right ones anyway. Even so, I hope the notes that follow convey, however imperfectly, just how grateful I am to the many people who have assisted me on this journey.

Considering that this book's intellectual roots reach back to my graduate-student years at the University of Michigan, there is only one way to begin: by thanking Rick Hall, a mentor and friend since the day I met him. When I first asked Rick about a potential study of presidential–congressional interactions during a walk across campus, he stopped and declared (with typical enthusiasm), "This would make an absolutely terrific dissertation topic." Better still, he offered to help. Fortunately for me, his was not an idle promise. Day in and day out, in Ann Arbor and Washington, Rick shared his penetrating insights, shrewd advice, and generous praise. Suffice it to say, I hope, I will never forget his unwavering confidence that I could do this project or his unyielding encouragement that I should.

A multitude of other Michigan friends and colleagues also helped me think through important questions at critical junctures. On this score, Rob Van Houweling's contributions stand out. Rob's comments always cut to the heart of the theory and corresponding tests of it. Section 3.5 in Chapter 3, in particular, not only aims to answer questions Rob asked but also reflects his advice on how best to do so. Chris Achen, Edie Goldenberg, Mike Hanmer, Vince Hutchings, John Jackson, Don Kinder, Ken Kollman, Greg Markus, Kris Miler, Mike

Traugott, and Nick Valentino were also instrumental in my thinking in different ways, at different times.

As important as my time at the University of Michigan was for nurturing this study at an early phase, its maturity came during my time at the University of California, Irvine (UCI). Vimal Kumar forced me to revisit important theoretical elements, while Bernie Grofman and Marty Wattenberg proved to be invaluable sounding boards on everything from the substantive to the logistic. I am grateful to all of them. Of course, their help would have been for naught had it not been for the extraordinary UCI students whose diligence generated the archival data that anchor this book. They are Carolyn Abdenour, Colleen Awad, Stefanie Boltz, Dannielle Evans, Lara Fong, Sarah Fuller, Lisa Haun, Zena Kalioundji, Cliff Kuehn, Sara Kunitake, Danni Menard, Jeff Post, Billy Ravel, Austin Rogers, Scott Seekatz, Taige Tan, Danny Tipton, and Bobby Zullo. The six months we worked together was the most rewarding time of my professional life – as fun and interesting as it was productive and insightful – and I appreciate every one of them for making it so.

Even though the presidential–congressional field has grown substantially, it retains the feel of a small community. Luckily for me, it is a supportive one as well. Time and again, various scholars have gone out of their way to offer constructive critiques, useful advice, and friendly encouragement. My thankfulness thus extends to Jon Bond, Jeff Cohen, Cary Covington, Gary Cox, George Edwards III, Richard Fleisher, Sam Kernell, Dave Lewis, Ken Mayer, Mat McCubbins, Jeff Peake, Russ Renka, Terry Sullivan, and Jim Thurber. I also hasten to add my thanks to the anonymous reviewers whose comments improved this book in ways big and small.

Inasmuch as the pages that follow include interesting insights on presidential–congressional relations, it speaks to scores of White House and congressional staffers' generosity. In fact, I remain amazed that busy officials were willing not only to answer my questions (and fill out my forms) but also to offer far more – from a private tour of the White House to a working breakfast at the Hay Adams Hotel. Confidentiality agreements do not allow me to thank them by name, so instead let me thank collectively the numerous officials who selflessly shared with a young, unconnected academic.

Several entities have contributed generously to my work. The Everett Dirksen Congressional Research Center and University of Michigan's Gerald R. Ford Fellowship allowed me to conduct the labor-intensive interviews just noted. Subsequent awards from UCI and UCI's Center for the Study of Democracy allowed me to gather additional data and then write up the results. I appreciate their support. Mark Petracca, my department chair, also allowed timely flexibility in my teaching schedule that greatly facilitated my writing. And I will be forever indebted to Ed Parsons for his help in marshaling this book to publication. My experience with Cambridge University Press has been nothing short of terrific, and that reflects Ed's wonderful combination of sound counsel and affable support.

Finally, and most importantly: my family. I sometimes joke that although I grew up in Southern California, I was raised as a Midwesterner. The reason is that my Mom and Dad (sometimes called Mary Lou and Bob) are modest, hardworking, caring people who thought that nothing was more interesting or important than their kids. The more I learn, the more I realize how much they taught, often without saying a word. So Mom and Dad, let me say here what I have said before and will again: I cannot thank you enough, and I love you more than you can imagine. This book is dedicated to you. I also thank Ben, my brother, for his loving support and timely laughs.

As for Kenya, my beautiful wife, what can I say? Attempting to enumerate the ways in which you have supported this project would be impossible; to do so beyond that would be laughable. Instead, let me just say that I love you with all my heart, and I cherish you for making the journey so much fun. Your love makes me want to be the best I can be, and your example helps show me the way. From the bottom of my heart, thank you.

And lastly, Weston, Brooks, and Charlotte, thank you for your smiles and steps, words and jumps, hugs, kisses, and silly faces. You each provide a compelling excuse to set aside all things political science, as well as the motivation to pick them back up. I am just grateful that I get to share in your lives. I love you all so much.

CHAPTER ONE

Introduction

In his Farewell Address to a nascent nation, George Washington admonished its future leaders to "confine themselves within their respective constitutional spheres, avoiding in the exercise of the powers of one department to encroach upon another." For better or worse, contemporary chief executives have ignored their forefather's advice. From the day they are elected till the day they leave office, today's presidents not only propose legislation addressing the nation's biggest problems but also undertake elaborate campaigns to promote its passage. What's more, American citizens expect, if not demand, that their presidents adopt this forward-leaning legislative posture.

Yet advocating legislation is far different from signing it, and rare is the case where presidents find coalition building on Capitol Hill easy. To shepherd a policy initiative to passage, a president not only must secure approval across myriad decision-making venues, in two chambers, and among 535 independent legislators but also must navigate a precarious undercurrent of competing agendas, limited time, scarce monies, diverse constituencies, entrenched interests, and parliamentary machinations. Perhaps it comes as no surprise, then, that grand designs for presidential leadership quickly give way to more sober realities. Ronald Reagan's quip captures the sentiment: "I have wondered at times what the Ten Commandments would have looked like if Moses had run them through the U.S. Congress."

The ominous path to signing ceremonies notwithstanding, presidents have continued to propose and promote an ambitious legislative agenda. As a matter of fact, policy-minded presidents have cited Congress' intractable instincts as evidence that their leadership is essential to effective lawmaking. No less an astute observer than Woodrow Wilson (1885) explained: "The Constitution bids [the President] speak, and times of stress and change must more and more thrust upon him the attitude of originator of policies," adding, "His is the vital place of action in the system, whether he accept it as such or not." Three-quarters of a century later, John F. Kennedy asserted much the same: the country needs presidents "who will formulate and fight for legislative policies, not be a casual bystander to the legislative process" (14 January 1960). Certainly no president since has disagreed.

The overriding question of presidents' legislative leadership, therefore, is not a question of resolve; it is a question of strategy: By what means can presidents build winning coalitions for their legislative agenda? Or as Richard Neustadt (1990 [1960], 4) aptly characterized it: "Strategically, the question is not how [the president] masters Congress in a peculiar instance, but what he does to boost his chance for mastery in any instance." This book aims to answer Neustadt's enduring question.

The core of my argument holds that most presidential coalition building occurs before roll-call votes near, often without changing pivotal voters' preferences. In fact, by pushing particular issues onto the congressional calendar and then manipulating which proposals ultimately surface as alternatives, I submit that postwar presidents' foremost influence comes in the legislative earlygame, not the legislative endgame. Therefore, this book reveals that when promoting presidential initiatives, instead of cobbling together support among "centrist" lawmakers, the White House's best options for building winning coalitions often come from mobilizing leading allies, deterring leading opponents, and circumventing endgame floor fights altogether.

Developing presidential coalition building as a generalizable class of strategies is itself instructive, a way of bringing clarity to presidential–congressional dynamics that have previously appeared idiosyncratic, if not irrational. However, the study's biggest payoff comes not from identifying presidents' legislative *strategies* but rather from discerning their substantive *effects*. In realizing how presidents target congressional processes upstream (how bills get to the floor, if they do) to influence downstream policy outcomes (what passes or does not), we see that standard tests of presidential influence have missed most of it. Using original data and new analyses that account for the interrelationship between prevoting and voting stages of the legislative process, I find that presidents' legislative influence is real, often substantial, and, to date, greatly underestimated.

Toward a better understanding of the practice and potential of presidential leadership in U.S. lawmaking, then, what follows is an extended investigation into the factors that shape presidents' policymaking prospects, the strategies presidents can employ to influence them, and the conditions that determine when those efforts will succeed – or not.[1] Along the way, competing claims will be tested against an eclectic array of evidence drawn from archival records, elite interviews, and systematic coding of the last half-century's presidential–congressional interactions regarding important domestic policy issues.

1.1 NEVER EASY

Explaining how his perception of Congress changed after he moved farther down Pennsylvania Avenue, from Capitol Hill to the White House, John Kennedy portrayed a view most presidents would recognize:

> The fact is that I think the Congress looks more powerful sitting here than it did when I was there in the Congress.... When you are in Congress, you are one of a hundred in the Senate or one of 435 in the House ... but from here I look at Congress and I look at the collective power of the Congress ... and it is a substantial power. (17 December 1962)

Decades later, after his first meeting with congressional leaders as president-elect, George W. Bush articulated a similar sentiment, albeit more bluntly: "If this were a dictatorship, this would be a heck of a lot easier – just so long as I'm dictator" (Mitchell 2000).

[1] By specifying the nature of presidents' legislative influence, this book complements recent research showing that presidents may affect policy change by executive decree (see Cooper 2002; Howell 2003; Mayer 2001; Moe 1984; Moe and Howell 1999). In particular, this study explains why presidents regularly choose to work through the lawmaking process rather than around it.

Considering that presidents enjoy nothing like dictatorial powers, each is better understood as but one player in a multifaceted, high-stakes policymaking game (see especially Cameron 2000, chap. 3; Jones 1994; M. Peterson 1990). In this light, let me begin by pointing out some of the important factors that shape presidents' prospects for marshaling proposals through Congress.

1.1.1 Constitutional Constraints

One of the first "facts" America's founding fathers cited to support their actions, in declaring independence from Great Britain, was King George III's heavy-handed tactics for enacting new laws: "He has called together legislative bodies at places unusual, uncomfortable, and distant from the depository of their Public Records, for the sole purpose of fatiguing them into compliance with his measures." Suffice it to say that when, a few years later, many of these same revolutionaries turned to drafting the U.S. Constitution, enhancing the chief executive's lawmaking power was not among their concerns. Article I states their preference bluntly: "All legislative Powers herein granted shall be vested in a Congress of the United States, which shall consist of a Senate and House of Representatives."

Despite giving Congress ultimate control over lawmaking, the Constitution does still accord presidents a few explicit legislative powers: a strong "negative" power and several weak "positive" ones. The first of these – the negative power, the veto – is well known and rigorously studied. With the bar for overturning a president's veto placed so high (two-thirds of the members in each chamber must vote to enact the bill over the president's objections), the veto power gives presidents a compelling weapon to deploy in congressional negotiations, which research shows they use to good effect. Wielding vetoes and threats thereof, presidents have been able to extract concessions from an oppositional Congress, if not kill its initiatives outright (Cameron 2000; Kiewit and McCubbins 1991).

In stark contrast to its imposing negative power, flimsy are the presidency's constitutional levers for exerting positive power – that is, for moving laws toward the president's preferred position. Although the Constitution authorizes each president to "recommend . . . measures as he shall deem necessary and expedient" and call Congress into session when he sees fit (Article 2, Section 3), it does not require that lawmakers afford those measures any special consideration, or any consideration at all. What's more, unlike members of Congress, presidents cannot drop policy proposals in the hopper, make floor speeches, offer amendments, raise points of order, filibuster, invoke "holds," vote, or engage in any number of other activities legislators may perform. Constitutionally speaking, then, presidents are not legislators – in chief or otherwise.

But in denying presidents' potent constitutional options for advancing legislation, it is noteworthy that the nation's founding document does not prohibit presidents from finding alternative paths for exerting influence. And in contrast to many early presidents – the Whigs, in particular – modern presidents have aggressively sought out such extraconstitutional paths to presidential influence.[2] Actually, recent presidents (Franklin Roosevelt and beyond) have pointedly rebuffed subservient views and instead endorsed Teddy Roosevelt's (1985 [1913]) constitutional outlook: a president is permitted to act unless forbidden by "specific restrictions and prohibitions appearing in the Constitution or imposed by Congress under its constitutional power" (389). The practical implication is that although lawmakers ultimately decide the nation's laws, today's presidents routinely, unabashedly lobby congressional members about legislation under their consideration.

Plainly, the presidency was not designed to help its occupants legislate; rather, it was explicitly constructed so they would not. Despite a strong veto and modest proposal powers, Congress ultimately determines the nation's laws. When it comes to promoting and passing their legislative agenda, the Constitution offers presidents little encouragement, less guidance, and no help. Such was the backdrop that when President Bill Clinton turned to the Constitution to emphasize his power after suffering an electoral dubbing in the 1994 midterm election – "The President is relevant.... The Constitution gives me

---

[2] Interestingly, after Teddy Roosevelt challenged the conceptions of a compliant presidency, his successor, William Howard Taft (1975 [1916]), tried to reassert it, arguing, "There is no undefined residuum of power which |the president| can exercise because it seems to him to be in the public interest" (139–140). The White House itself suggests whose view won out. Adjacent to the Oval Office is the Roosevelt Room, named for two activist presidents: Teddy and Franklin Roosevelt. There is no Taft Room.

relevance" (18 April 1995) – pundits, pols, and political scientists alike interpreted it as underscoring his weakness.

1.1.2   Partisan (and Preference) Constraints

Unfortunately for White House officials, the Constitution is not the only obstacle darkening the legislative horizon; partisan realities further curb presidents' prospects for marshaling preferred initiatives to passage. As Richard Neustadt (1990 [1960]) observed fifty years back, "What the Constitution separates the parties do not combine" (33). This is so for at least two reasons. First, American citizens rarely flood their capital with one party's members. Over the last half-century, the partisan splits within Congress have tended to be relatively close, and between the White House and the Congress, divided government has existed far more often than not.

Table 1.1 lists the presidential party's percentage of seats in each chamber, from 1953 to 2004. As it shows, few presidents have enjoyed large partisan majorities in both houses; most have confronted a Congress with at least one chamber controlled by members of the opposing party. Furthermore, even presidents who entered office with especially strong partisan majorities in both the House and the Senate – for example, Presidents Kennedy, Johnson, and Carter – knew that Congress' (liberal) northern and (conservative) southern Democrats were different species, even though they shared the same class.

The second reason parties prove insufficient for providing presidents with a reliable voting bloc is hinted at in the first: the ties that bind presidents and their fellow partisans in Congress are important but far from unbreakable. Sharing a party label and a stake in its public reputation may engender some "team spirit" (see Cox and McCubbins 1993; Smith 2007), but ultimately lawmakers operate according to their individual self-interests (Jacobson 2000; Sinclair 2006; Wattenberg 1991, 1998). As such, legislators can (and do) turn away from their party's president when they believe he has chosen the wrong path. President Carter's tumultuous time in Washington underscores this reality. He wrote, "I learned the hard way that there was no party loyalty or discipline when a complicated or controversial issue was at stake – none. . . . It was every member for himself, and the devil take the hindmost!" (Carter 1995, 84).

TABLE 1.1. *Presidential party's percentage of seats in Congress, 1953–2004*

President	Congress (years)	Percentage of members in president's party	
		House	Senate
Eisenhower	83rd (1953–54)	51%	50%
Eisenhower	84th (1955–56)	47%	49%
Eisenhower	85th (1957–58)	46%	49%
Eisenhower	86th (1959–60)	35%	35%
Kennedy	87th (1961–62)	61%	64%
Kennedy/Johnson	88th (1963–64)	59%	67%
Johnson	89th (1965–66)	68%	68%
Johnson	90th (1967–68)	57%	64%
Nixon	91st (1969–70)	44%	42%
Nixon	92nd (1971–72)	41%	45%
Nixon/Ford	93rd (1973–74)	44%	43%
Ford	94th (1975–76)	33%	38%
Carter	95th (1977–78)	67%	62%
Carter	96th (1979–80)	64%	59%
Reagan	97th (1981–82)	44%	53%
Reagan	98th (1983–84)	38%	54%
Reagan	99th (1985–86)	42%	53%
Reagan	100th (1987–88)	41%	45%
Bush (41)	101st (1989–90)	40%	45%
Bush (41)	102nd (1991–92)	38%	44%
Clinton	103rd (1993–94)	59%	57%
Clinton	104th (1995–96)	46%	46%
Clinton	105th (1997–98)	47%	45%
Clinton	106th (1999–2000)	49%	45%
Bush (43)	107th (2001–2)	51%	50%
Bush (43)	108th (2002–4)	52%	51%

Several recent scholars have amplified President Carter's point of view. Building on the idea that a president's policymaking prospects turn less on Congress' partisan breakdown than lawmakers' preference distribution, Keith Krehbiel (1998) and Henry Brady and Craig Volden (1998) further theorize that presidents' congressional fortunes depend on specific "pivotal" voters' ideological outlook.

The crux of the pivotal politics model, depicted graphically in Figure 1.1, is that presidential initiatives require support from 218 representatives and 60 senators, so the president's legislative fate

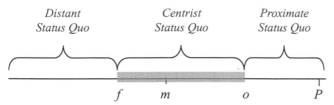

Figure 1.1 The Pivotal Politics Model of Lawmaking.

hangs with the legislators who cast those decisive votes. When facing a chamber whose members are ideologically aligned from liberal to conservative, success for a conservative president (P) seeking to replace some "distant" status quo (sq) – that is, one on the opposite side of the median (or pivotal) voter – depends on winning over the House's median voter (m) and the Senate's swing voter to overcome filibusters (f).[3]

Table 1.2 locates pivotal voters' ideological predispositions for the last half-century of president–Congress constellations using Keith Poole and Howard Rosenthal's (1997) estimates of congressional members' basic ideological outlook, ranging from –1 (extremely liberal) to +1 (extremely conservative). As it shows, the Senate's filibuster pivot – who happens to have always been the more disagreeable of the two pivotal voters – is almost always someone from the opposite side of the ideological divide. Of these ten presidents, only Jimmy Carter entered Washington with House and Senate pivotal voters who shared his basic ideological outlook, and barely even then. Every other president has found at least the Senate's swing voter predisposed toward opposition, with Presidents Ford, Reagan, and (post-1994) Clinton confronting particularly unsympathetic swing voters.

1.1.3 Contextual Constraints

Lacking a strong constitutional anchor, resilient partisan loyalties, or widespread ideological agreement, proactive presidents have instead had to utilize a less durable source of strength: persuasion. As Richard Neustadt (1990 [1960]) explained it, "Presidential 'powers' may be

---

[3] The Senate first introduced the cloture option for cutting off debate (Senate Rule 22) in 1917, which then required a two-thirds majority. In 1975, senators reduced the cloture threshold to a three-fifths supermajority (i.e., sixty votes).

TABLE 1.2. *Congressional pivotal voters' distance from the president,*
1953–2004

President	Congress (years)	Pivotal voter's distance from president[a]	
		House (median)	Senate (filibuster pivot)
Eisenhower	83rd (1953–54)	0.88	1.04
Eisenhower	84th (1955–56)	0.95	1.19
Eisenhower	85th (1957–58)	0.95	1.18
Eisenhower	86th (1959–60)	1.07	1.31
Kennedy	87th (1961–62)	1.00	1.16
Kennedy/Johnson	88th (1963–64)	1.00	1.08
Johnson	89th (1965–66)	0.85	1.09
Johnson	90th (1967–68)	1.01	1.08
Nixon	91st (1969–70)	1.00	1.31
Nixon	92nd (1971–72)	1.04	1.27
Nixon/Ford	93rd (1973–74)	1.04	1.34
Ford	94th (1975–76)	1.19	1.35
Carter	95th (1977–78)	0.83	0.93
Carter	96th (1979–80)	0.86	0.95
Reagan	97th (1981–82)	1.05	1.13
Reagan	98th (1983–84)	1.12	1.15
Reagan	99th (1985–86)	1.10	1.16
Reagan	100th (1987–88)	1.11	1.23
Bush (41)	101st (1989–90)	1.12	1.25
Bush (41)	102nd (1991–92)	1.14	1.26
Clinton	103rd (1993–94)	0.85	1.00
Clinton	104th (1995–96)	1.19	1.25
Clinton	105th (1997–98)	1.18	1.29
Clinton	106th (1999–2000)	1.16	1.29
Bush (43)	107th (2001–2)	0.82	1.30
Bush (43)	108th (2002–4)	0.76	1.27

[a] Ideological distance scaled from 0 to 2, based on estimates from all members' roll-call voting behavior (see Poole and Rosenthal 1997).

inconclusive when a President commands, but always remain relevant as he persuades" (30). This – the recognition that presidential power turns more on effective bargaining than on institutional prerogative – was Neustadt's seminal insight.

Yet presidential persuasion does not occur in a vacuum, and its effectiveness is anything but categorical. In contrast to constitutional options like the veto, which is always viable, persuasive pitches and

bargaining appeals work only inasmuch as those on the receiving
end are willing to listen and respond thereafter. Again, Richard
Neustadt (1990 [1960]) expressed the point artfully: "Persuasion
deals in the coin of self-interest with men who have some freedom
to reject what they find counterfeit" (40). Subsequent work has built
from Neustadt's base to specify how various macro-level "contexts"
help determine when congressional members will deem a president's
micro-level appeals compelling, and when they will reject them as
counterfeit.

1.1.3.1   Historical context. Among the contexts that presidents inhabit
and that condition members' responsiveness, the most elemental is
what Stephen Skowronek (1993) calls the president's "political time" –
a function of his position vis-à-vis the dominant regime (an amalgam of
the prevailing governing philosophy coupled with its partisan embod-
iment) and the public's view of it. Presidents who challenge the dominant regime as it falls into public disrepute will have ample opportunities to wield influence. "Presidents stand preeminent in American
politics when government has been most thoroughly discredited, and
when political resistance to the presidency is weakest, presidents tend
to remake government wholesale" (37). Presidents whose historical moment led other officials to defer to their leadership include
Abraham Lincoln and Franklin Roosevelt.

On the other end of the congressional receptivity spectrum, according to Skowronek (1993), are presidents who either support a "discredited" regime or oppose a "resilient" one. These presidents, including
Herbert Hoover and Jimmy Carter, will find occasions for legislative
success rare and fleeting, as they are "consumed by a problem that is
really prerequisite to leadership, that of establishing any credibility at
all" (39). Indeed, presidents operating in such unfavorable "political
times" get tagged as being out of touch, or even incompetent, and are
largely ignored as a consequence.

At the broadest level, then, presidents' prospects for exerting
influence are shaped by the political-historical moment they happen to occupy (see also Lewis and Strine 1996). Presidents in favorable political-historical circumstances find other Washington officials
willing to follow their lead; presidents in unfavorable moments do

not.[4] But if "political time" sets the basic strategic parameters for presidential leadership, it is other situational features that more directly constrain a president's day-in, day-out tactical opportunities (see Dickinson 2008; Lieberman 2000). Briefly let me introduce the most important of these circumstantial constraints.

1.1.3.2 Political context. Political theorists have long cited competitive elections as a properly functioning republic's lynchpin – the essential mechanism by which "the people" retain ultimate control of their government, its officials, and the nation's laws (see Dahl 1956; Pitkin 1967). But elections' centrality in American democracy extends far beyond abstract concerns of representation and accountability. To be sure, public officials' attention to any "messages" citizens send via their votes is anything but abstract; elections are a daily consideration as members anticipate how best to keep their jobs (Arnold 1990; Fenno 1978; Kingdon 1989; Mayhew 1974).[5] Given elections' centrality in lawmakers' decision making, practitioners and pundits alike have argued that presidents' electoral standing affects members' response to their appeals, especially during their "honeymoon" and "lame duck" periods.

The early months of a president's first term provide high times for those inside the West Wing. Buoyed by an election-induced fusion among the president, his policies, and the public, administrations tend to enjoy unusual support in Congress early on (see Beckmann and Godfrey 2007; P. Conley 2001; Grossback, Peterson, and Stimson 2005; D. Peterson et al. 2003). This honeymoon success is bolstered when, as often happens, the president's partisan opponents hold their fire, thereby affording the president favorable news coverage and, in turn, favorable poll numbers (see Brace and Hinkley

---

4 In many ways, Skowronek's "political time" is recast as the status quo position in my model. In fact, like Skowronek's theory, my model predicts that the more distant the status quo policy (from the president's ideal), the better the president's prospects for replacing it with one of his own.
5 While many scholars have debunked the notion that voters can offer a "mandate" using an instrument as imprecise as their vote (see especially Dahl 1990; Wolfinger 1985), others have argued that elections can, at least, signal the majority's directional preference vis-à-vis the status quo (see P. Conley 2001; Fiorina 1981; D. Peterson et al. 2003; Rabinowitz and Macdonald 1989).

1992; Brody 1991; Grossman and Kumar 1981). Paul Light (1999) thus emphasized how the honeymoon – "the early grace period of grace and good humor" (45) – offers presidents an especially receptive audience on Capitol Hill compared to what they will find in subsequent years.[6]

If the presidential honeymoon leaves lawmakers particularly receptive to the president's pitches, the opposite is often said of the president's lame duck period – the final year of a president's second term, when he will inhabit neither the ballot in November nor the Oval Office come January. Accordingly, many have argued that presidents' influence wanes as their tenure comes to a close (see Light 1999), though presidents themselves have objected to such claims. President Eisenhower explained, "I have not noticed any effect of the so-called 'lame duck.' Maybe later in the term that might be noticeable. To me, it is not now" (7 August 1957). President Clinton answered simply "Yes" when asked, "Isn't that expression 'lame duck' a painful one?" (15 March 1999).

Of course, political context remains important between the beginning and the end of an administration, the honeymoon and lame duck periods. Pollster Patrick Caddell emphasized this point in a private memo to President Jimmy Carter: "Essentially, it is my thesis governing with public approval requires a continuing political campaign," to which Carter replied, "Excellent" (*Time*, 30 October 2005). Political scientists, however, have found such claims substantially overblown. While presidents' "going public" campaigns may help influence Congress when the president (see Brace and Hinckley 1992; Kernell 1993; Neustadt 1990 [1960], chap. 5) and/or his policies (see Canes-Wrone 2005; Canes-Wrone and de Marchi 2002) are popular, such influence is modest at best (see Bond, Fleisher, and Krutz 1996; Bond and Fleisher 1990, 2000; Edwards 1989; Krehbiel 1998). Also, research shows that presidents have little ability to dramatically change

---

[6] One point is worth underscoring: electoral honeymoons provide presidents with an opportunity for early legislative success, not a guarantee. Bill Clinton's turbulent first months in office generally, and on Capitol Hill in particular, highlight the distinction. Speaking to a newlywed reporter during his first summer in the White House, President Clinton joked, "You know what I'm really upset about? You got a honeymoon, and I didn't" (15 June 1993).

the public's prevailing opinion, which is rooted more in the country's fundamentals – especially peace and prosperity – than the particulars of the president's message or its packaging (see Edwards 1983, 2003; Fiorina 1981; Kramer 1983; Page and Shapiro 1992).

1.1.3.3 "Real-world" context. Finally, beyond the broader historical and political contexts that shape each president's persuasive potential, one additional contextual feature is important but often overlooked: presidents operate in a world they do not control. "Real-world" events like *Brown v. Board of Education of Topeka* (1954), *Sputnik* (1957), the assassination of Martin Luther King, Jr. (1968), Watergate (1972), the Stock Market Crash (1987), the fall of the Berlin Wall (1989), Monica Lewinsky (1998), and 9/11 (2001), not to mention the wars in Korea (1950–53), Vietnam (approx. 1959–75), and Iraq (1990–91, 2003–present), all affect presidents' persuasive potential in Congress. They do so, first, by diverting presidents' energies away from congressional politics and, second, by either boosting (as after the September 11th attacks) or undercutting (as after the Nixon pardon) Washington officials' attention and receptivity to the president's appeals.

1.2 PRESIDENTIAL SKILL, STRATEGY, AND SUCCESS

As we have just seen, its signal role in American politics notwithstanding, the presidency offers its occupants no obvious options for translating preferred initiatives into public laws. Because they operate within the confines of a Constitution and context they largely inherit and cannot change, that presidents find congressional lawmaking uncomfortably confining is understandable. A few years into his administration, Franklin Roosevelt recalled how his cousin Teddy (Roosevelt) once declared, "Sometimes I wish I could be President and Congress too." After a brief pause, FDR added, "Well, I suppose if the truth were told, he is not the only President that has had that idea" (12 June 1936).

But highly constrained is not wholly constrained; opportunities for presidents to overcome congressional inclinations always arise. Presidential leadership in lawmaking does not require imposing one's will against all odds; rather, it entails identifying strategic opportunities in Congress, divining ways to capitalize on them, and then executing those strategies effectively. Or, as George Edwards (1989) succinctly stated it, "The essential presidential skill in leading Congress is in recognizing and exploiting conditions for change, not creating them" (221; see also, Peterson 1990).

Despite ample attention on these core aspects of presidential leadership – that is, recognizing and exploiting strategic legislative opportunities – broadly applicable theories have thus far proven elusive. Still unclear are the opportunities presidents have for exerting influence; still unspecified are the strategies presidents have for exploiting those opportunities. And lacking a clear theory that explains presidents' strategic opportunities and tactical choices, many a practitioner and pundit have instead surmised that president-led coalition building requires something of a heroic personal skill. Let me quickly point out the limitations of such personalized explanations before introducing the theory at the heart of this book – one that puts positive presidential power on firmer conceptual footing.

1.2.1 Beyond "Skill"

Coming on the heels of Franklin Roosevelt's historic time in office, initial scholarly appraisals largely mirrored Woodrow Wilson's (1917 [1981]) famous depiction of presidential power: "The President is at liberty, both in law and conscience, to be as big a man as he can" and "his office is anything he has the sagacity and force to make it" (69). Like Wilson, these earlier researchers assumed that the presidency's discretionary nature left its occupants' policymaking possibilities wide open, which, in turn, led to the inference that each president's legislative accomplishments hinged on the president himself – his character, his acumen, his effectiveness (Barber 1972; Burns 1965; Corwin 1957; Greenstein 1982; Rossiter 1956; Schlesinger 1973; Sperlich 1975; see also Kellerman 1984). James MacGregor Burns's take (in a 1965 tome entitled *Presidential Government: The Crucible of Leadership*) is typical of the genre:

> Better than any other human instrumentality [a president] can order the relations of his ends and means, alter existing institutions and procedures or create new ones, calculate the consequences of

different policies, experiment with various methods, control the tim-
ing of action, anticipate the reactions of affected interests, and con-
ciliate them or at least mediate among them. (339)

Conceptualized as such, presidential coalition building surfaces as
something of an intangible instinct, an extraordinary skill. And, of
course, this is precisely how presidential lobbying gets treated in news
stories, personal memoirs, and presidential biographies. Anthony
King (1983) summarized this popular view:

> There is easy agreement about wherein the relevant elements of a
> president's personality and political skills lie: warmth, accessibility,
> an intimate knowledge of the workings of Congress, sensitivity to
> congressmen's power stakes as well as his own, a willingness to work
> with congressional leaders, a willingness to talk with members with a
> view to finding out what is on their minds as well as telling them what
> is on his own, a shrewd instinct for timing, knowledge of whom to
> bully and whom not to bully, a capacity for remembering who might
> like to use the White House tennis court – and so on into the middle
> distance. (252)

However, as already discussed, subsequent inquiry has refuted the
thesis that presidential power is personally derived. We now know that
if presidents' personal "skill" plays a part in their legislative influence,
it is far from a central part.[7] Again, constitutional edicts and political
context delimit what a president can achieve – occasionally for better,
often for worse.

Yet the finding that presidents' personal skills cannot override congressional predispositions does not mean that presidents lack influence on Capitol Hill. To be sure, still unclear is the more basic question: Can presidents systematically identify and methodically exploit
opportunities to induce lawmakers to pass something different than

---

[7] Actually, contemporary researchers have explicitly eschewed "president-centered"
theories, instead preferring "presidency-centered" ones (see Moe 1993). The argument is that all presidents behave rationally and, thus, execute similar strategies in
the face of comparable challenges (Edwards 1989; Hager and Sullivan 1994; Jones
1994). Then again, John Gilmour (2002) reminds us that "similar" is not "the same,"
with the difference remaining potentially decisive in any particular case.

they otherwise would? So what remains unresolved is not the importance (or unimportance) of presidential "skill" but rather the importance (or unimportance) of presidential "strategy." This is a point Barbara Sinclair has noted, and one that led her to recommend further study of the latter (see also Cameron 2000, chap. 3). Writing that "[the] labeling of leaders as strong or weak is unproblematical but also not in and of itself particularly enlightening," Sinclair (1993, 205) instead suggests the following:

> If conceptualized in terms of observable behavior and activities, leadership style becomes a variable upon which some agreement among scholars and across leaders may be possible. . . . Students of the presidency, like students of congressional party leadership, are interested in what the holders of the position do, why they do it, and with what effect. Given that interest, the argument for focusing on concrete observable variables such as activities or decisions seems very strong. (206–7)

I agree. Understanding what presidents and their staffers actually do to forge winning coalitions for their legislative initiatives is integral to assessing the practice and potential of presidential leadership in lawmaking. In developing and executing a legislative strategy, presidents and their aides reveal the opportunities they see for passing presidents' proposals, as well as the tactics they deem effective for capitalizing on those opportunities. Tracing these strategies thus shows how they are intended to work and, in turn, offers a clearer blueprint for assessing whether they do. While the chapters that follow offer an in-depth treatment along these lines, it is useful to briefly introduce the argument here as well.

1.2.2   The Strategies of Presidential Influence

When the Senate resoundingly rejected President George H. W. Bush's proposed budget "deal" from a few days earlier, reporters wondered aloud about the White House's legislative incompetence. Asked whether he had "taken any of [his] staff to the woodshed" for performing poorly, President Bush objected, saying, "In terms of my team, they did an outstanding job. And I've had more Members tell me that. So, what you hear is the squeaking wheel," to which one reporter offered a salty retort: "Who, sir, are these Members of Congress who are hailing the work of your team?" (9 October 1990).[8]

Even though Washington correspondents surely overestimate a sitting president's potential sway in Congress, more than a kernel of truth remains. Modern presidents do enjoy tremendous persuasive assets: unmatched public visibility, unequaled professional staff, unrivaled historical prestige, unparalleled fundraising capacity. And buttressing these persuasive power sources are others, including a president's considerable discretion over federal appointments, bureaucratic rules, legislative vetoes, and presidential trinkets.[9] So even with their limitations duly noted, presidents clearly still enjoy an impressive bounty in the grist of political persuasion – one they can (and do) draw on to help build winning coalitions on Capitol Hill.

But how? That is, how can a president best allocate his persuasive arsenal to influence Congress and, in turn, the nation's laws? The core of my argument, introduced here and developed fully in Chapter 2, is that building on a singular ability to propel initiatives onto the legislative calendar (i.e., agenda setting), modern chief executives can further promote their proposals per two lobbying strategies: a vote-centered strategy aimed at winning the congressional endgame directly and an agenda-centered strategy aimed at winning before then. Briefly let me foreshadow these basic strategic elements and the presidential–congressional compounds they help explain.

1.2.2.1 Presidential agenda setting. The first path by which presidents may influence Congress is also the most widely recognized: the presidency gives its occupants an incomparable capacity to develop and

---

[8] Similarly, legislative successes are portrayed as reflecting a president's deftness. Whereupon Ronald Reagan signed the landmark Tax Reform Act of 1986 into law, the corresponding article in *The New York Times* concluded that, while others were involved, "no one doubts that the President deserves primary credit and responsibility for the new tax system" (23 October 1986).

[9] Beltway insiders, for instance, often cite the importance of personal favors, such as presidents' ability to offer lawmakers tickets to the president's box at the Kennedy Center, travel aboard *Air Force One*, invitations to state dinners, tours of the White House residence, seats for movie premieres in the White House movie theater, and drinks on the Truman Balcony. Speaker Tip O'Neill once lamented, "There aren't two White Houses.... [An invitation to] have lunch with the Speaker or sit in the Speaker's gallery just isn't in the same league" (Dewar 1981).

publicize policy initiatives – in other words, to set the national policy agenda. Recognizing this potential is what inspired Theodore Roosevelt to label the presidency a "bully pulpit."

The most basic foundation beneath presidents' agenda-setting ability is that developing legislative initiatives is hard work. Major legislation is often as thick as a set of encyclopedias, and Herculean is the workload entailed in, say, reforming Medicare, reconfiguring the nation's energy system, rewriting the tax code, or revising welfare policies. Because resources used to address one issue come at the expense of others, not to mention nonlegislative matters politicians care about (like fundraising and campaigning), the ability to invest heavily in one policy domain is a luxury few policymakers enjoy (Arnold 1991; Hall 1996; Kingdon 1989). Here, modern presidents stand out. Supported by both White House staff and a massive federal bureaucracy, nobody can match a president's access to expertise or control over man-hours (see Burke 1992; Dickinson 1997; Ponder 2000; Rudalevige 2002; Walcott and Hult 1995; Warshaw 1997). Citing the administration's informational advantages vis-à-vis lawmakers, Andrew Rudalevige (2002) noted, "Congress may not always be inclined to dispose, but presidents are now very much expected to propose" (2).

Beyond the ability to draft comprehensive policy proposals, today's chief executives also enjoy an unrivaled platform for drawing citizens' attention to those initiatives.[10] Not only is the president the country's most widely recognized public official, but also his office affords a myriad of institutional resources for advertising his legislative agenda, such as the annual State of the Union address (J. Cohen 1997), ad hoc press conferences or speeches (Hager and Sullivan 1994; Kernell 1993), and a sizable staff to support those and other "going public" activities (see J. Cohen 2008; Grossman and Kumar 1981; Kumar 2007; Patterson 2000). All of these assets help an administration tap presidents' incomparable, albeit still limited, ability to attract media attention – both nationally (Edwards and Wood 1999; Gans 1979; but

---

[10] So despite the fact that presidents cannot substantially change the public's policy preferences (as discussed previously), they can increase citizens' awareness of an issue and the president's proposal to address it (as discussed here).

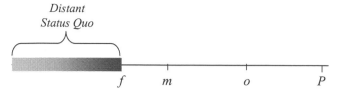

Figure 1.2 Presidents' Legislative Influence via Agenda Setting.

see Baum and Kernell 1999) and locally (Barrett and Peake 2007; Cohen 2009) – which can further bolster the importance citizens assign to the president's priority issues (Iyengar and Kinder 1987).

Owing to their extraordinary capacity to draft and advocate policy proposals, postwar presidents have been exceedingly effective at getting their key initiatives onto the congressional calendar. George Edwards and Andrew Barrett's (2000) detailed study of presidential proposals showed that virtually all of them – 97.6 percent to be exact – were at least subjected to a congressional hearing. Similarly, Gary Cox and Mathew McCubbins (2005) found that when the House's majority party was "rolled," it was almost always because the opposing party's president pushed his bills onto the congressional calendar, the Speaker's objections notwithstanding. Even a credible signal that the president will advocate an issue can be sufficient to push it onto lawmakers' docket (Canes-Wrone 2005; Kingdon 1989, 1995).

Drawing on the pivotal-politics model discussed earlier, Figure 1.2 illustrates how presidents' agenda-setting potential allows them to influence legislation. By inducing congressional consideration of a particular status quo, the president can change the law from some distant policy position ($sq < f$) to one closer to his ideal (to f).[11] Notice that this influence occurs even if the president cannot convince a single member to change his or her predisposition on the issue. So even if the old saw were true – "the president proposes and the Congress disposes" – the ability to get lawmakers to address some status

---

[11] Importantly, for a president to actually *influence* Congress via agenda setting, the situation must be that the issue would otherwise go unaddressed, the status quo unaltered. If some exogenous shock induces lawmakers to consider an issue independent of its relationship to the president, then any correlation between a president's "going public" activities and Congress' consideration is spurious. I discuss the empirical implications for estimating presidential influence in greater detail later.

quo (that would otherwise go unaddressed) gives presidents a real and potentially substantial influence on lawmaking, especially in times of divided government, when his bills would otherwise be blocked from reaching the floor (see R. Conley 2003; Cox and McCubbins 2005; Cox and Katz 2007; but see Mayhew 2005).

1.2.2.2 Presidential lobbying. Of course, not since Calvin Coolidge has a chief executive been content merely to propose bills and sign whatever legislation Congress happens to send back. Today's presidents want to exert influence beyond agenda setting and, to this end, undertake elaborate lobbying campaigns to solicit lawmakers' support. It is a posture that Theodore Roosevelt and Woodrow Wilson advocated, and one that all presidents since Dwight Eisenhower have institutionalized with a team of full-time lobbyists in the Executive Office of the President (see Collier 1997). Harry Truman articulated the now familiar outlook: "The legislative job of the President is especially important.... I sometimes express it by saying the President is the only lobbyist that [most] Americans have" (25 October 1956).[12]

Still, as presidents already know or quickly learn, attempting influence is not the same as exerting it. As a matter of fact, White House staffers consider the distinction between effort and impact so crucial that they devote impressive amounts of time to devising, monitoring, and implementing so-called legislative strategy. The question they ask, issue after issue, day after day, is deceptively simple: By what means can we best build a winning congressional coalition for the president's preferred policy? In practice, this translates into *Whom should we lobby?* and *How should we lobby them?* The strategies that inspire the White House's answers form the crux of presidents' legislative options, and implementing them effectively comprises the basis of presidents' positive influence.

---

[12] It is worth noting that agenda setting and lobbying are not mutually exclusive. As John Kingdon (1995) noted, "Official Washington has developed very sensitive antennae for measuring the subtleties of a presidential commitment. A president can mention an item in the State of the Union Address or in another public forum, but participants look for signs of commitment beyond the pro forma mention – phone calls, repeated requests to take up the issue, signs of actually using such powers of the office as the veto or the publicity advantages" (26).

In the political scientist's typical formulation, presidential aides' choices of lobbying targets and tactics should prove fairly straightforward. Because the White House's essential task is winning floor roll-call votes, especially "key" votes, most research presumes that presidents' lobbying efforts are aimed at Congress' swing voters (see Brady and Volden 1998; Covington 1986, 1987, 1988; Covington, Wrighton, and Kinney, 1995; Krehbiel 1998; Lockerbie, Borrelli, and Hedger 1998; Pritchard 1983; Rivers and Rose 1985; Sullivan 1988, 1991). And, sure enough, strategizing how to pull potentially pivotal voters toward the president's position is standard fare in the West Wing, as is executing tactics intended to achieve that objective. This *vote-centered strategy* aims to win the congressional endgame directly by shifting members' preference distribution on roll-call votes. As noted, the logic of this vote-centered strategy offers clear operational advice: lobby the pivotal voters with all the tactical arrows in the president's persuasive quiver.

But as important as presidents' endgame plays for pivotal members' votes can be, they do not capture the full spectrum of presidents' coalition-building activities. Indeed, I argue that vote-centered lobbying typically serves to complement the White House's second more potent lobbying option: bargaining with congressional leaders over the alternatives subject to votes. Per this *agenda-centered strategy*, presidential staffers work with leading congressional allies to advocate the president's preferred policy while simultaneously inducing leading opponents not to challenge key provisions therein. When successfully executed, the White House's agenda-centered lobbying strategy backs pivotal voters into an unsavory choice: supporting a president-backed policy "deal" or doing nothing at all. By permitting presidents to focus their resources on a handful of congressional leaders (rather than spreading them across a band of pivotal voters), agenda-centered lobbying offers presidents a distinct and valuable path for passing legislation – one that has been underspecified when not overlooked altogether.[13]

---

[13] While scholars have long recognized the potential for a savvy agenda setter to engineer policy alternatives to his or her advantage (Arrow 1951; Grofman 2004; Kingdon 1995; McKelvey 1976; Romer and Rosenthal 1978), the presumption has been that such manipulations are not particularly relevant to presidential–congressional

$$f \qquad f' \qquad o \qquad P$$

Figure 1.3 Presidents' Legislative Influence via Lobbying.

Although precisely exposing the policy returns on presidents' strategic lobbying investments requires a detailed theoretical treatment, the basic design can already be seen. Figure 1.3 illustrates how presidents' lobbying influence is realized in terms of legislation in cases where presidents target their lobbying resources to replacing dispreferred status quos with policies closer to their own ideal. Again drawing from the pivotal-politics model described previously, absent any presidential lobbying or influence, policies that are far off the status quo will be amended to reflect the filibuster pivot's predisposition (f). But with the smart choice and effective execution of vote-centered and/or agenda-centered lobbying strategies, the president can push the policy outcome from that default position (f) to one closer to his ideal (f').

1.2.3   The Keys to Success (or Locks on Failure)

Beyond clarifying exactly what options presidents have for advocating legislation, an additional insight is gained from tracking these strategies further: we see the factors that condition their effectiveness. So although the basic strategic blueprint applies generally across presidents and Congresses, its potential effectiveness depends on the players involved, the policy implicated, and the political context. Again, Chapter 2 derives and explains this in the context of a unified theory, but it is useful to foreshadow the highlights here.

1.2.3.1   The status quo. Earlier, I distinguished among three status quo locations vis-à-vis the president – distant, centrist, and proximate – and explained how each determines a president's prospects for passing an alternative to it. Presidents who tackle a legislative landscape dense with "distant" status quos are likely to enjoy legislative success; those working amid "centrist" or "proximate" status quo policies will have

---

interactions. Writing of the potential for presidential or congressional agenda manipulation, Keith Krehbiel (1998), for example, writes, "Such plans are much easier to envision than they are to execute" (228).

a harder time convincing Congress' pivotal voters to replace them with the president's. Then again, it only takes a few distant status quos for the White House to find a profitable set of policy targets. Consequently, knowing how legislators, especially pivotal voters, feel about "doing nothing" offers the first key to predicting a president's legislative destiny.

1.2.3.2 Supportive leaders' preferences. When anticipating how a presidential proposal will fare on Capitol Hill, White House officials must consider not only obvious challenges but also those that are less than obvious. One of these insidious threats comes from a president's own congressional leaders. When the president's party leaders share his preferences or are willing to subjugate their own, the president can be sure his initiatives will get strong advocacy and substantial support. Typically, this is exactly what happens. However, when the president and his side's congressional leaders disagree, stalemate may be the best outcome the president can achieve.

1.2.3.3 Opposing leaders' preferences. Whereupon the president and his congressional allies coalesce around a particular policy, which they usually will, leading opponents must then decide how to respond. Should they fight for their own policy proposal? Should they look to compromise with the White House? Should they filibuster or otherwise obstruct? Or should they just keep their powder dry and focus their efforts elsewhere? The answers to these questions depend, in part, on the opposing leaders' preferences. The more disagreeable and the less pliable the opposing side's leaders, the more likely they will choose confrontation over conciliation and, perhaps, even compromise. Conversely, if the president happens to face moderate and/or persuadable leading opponents, the White House may not merely strike a deal with these leading opponents but actually achieve a policy outcome better than would have been possible if the administration had focused all energies at securing pivotal voters' support.

1.2.3.4 Pivotal voters' preferences. At the end of the day, roll-call votes settle legislative debates. Like previous theories, then, the one developed here stresses the importance of floor votes and the pivotal voters who decide them. In my account, pivotal voters matter directly whenever close, contested votes approach, and they matter indirectly whenever presidents and congressional leaders anticipate how to prevail on such votes. The consequence is that pivotal voters' preferences, including their flexibility in response to presidential pressure, greatly affect a president's chances for experiencing success, failure, or something in between. Perhaps it comes as no surprise, therefore, that among a president's most important acolytes are those who can accurately estimate legislators' (voting) cards before they are required to show their hands.

1.2.3.5 The president's political capital. The final piece of the theoretical puzzle developed here emphasizes the variability in presidents' persuasiveness. Some presidents, at some times, find lawmakers especially responsive to their soft sells and hard bargains; other presidents, at other times, do not. Again, this has far less to do with each president's personal characteristics or rhetorical punch than it does with his particular political circumstances. Presidents operating amid a strong economy and popular support will, I argue, find lawmakers more malleable than presidents bogged down by a flagging economy and disapproving public.

1.3   GOING FORWARD

Having introduced its theoretical nucleus here, in the rest of this book I turn to further specifying presidents' coalition-building options, their optimal choice among them, and the expected effects on legislation. Chapter 2 does just this, teasing out the full theory of presidential influence, from getting particular issues on Congress' docket (agenda setting) to promoting them when there (lobbying). It explains how presidential coalition building sometimes requires last-minute lobbying for votes but, more often, entails rallying leading allies and deterring leading opponents. Part and parcel of this argument is showing how familiar conceptions of presidents' influence mischaracterize the ways in which it is exerted, as well as the ways in which it is manifested.

After the logic motivating presidents' lobbying campaigns has been detailed, the first empirical follow-up question is clear: Do presidents and their advisors actually execute those strategies? Chapter 3 tests the theoretical tenets of presidential lobbying – the on-the-ground behaviors by which presidents and their aides are predicted to exert influence in Congress. Because most presidential–congressional interactions occur in private, among surrogates, and without any systematic record, gathering valid data on White House lobbying requires collecting it from the people involved. To test the White House's lobbying efforts, therefore, the data used in this chapter come from elite interviews with White House and Senate officials about their interactions regarding President George W. Bush's 2001 tax cut proposal. The results corroborate the theory and its principal hypotheses; they show that the administration targeted their persuasive arsenal primarily at congressional leaders, while also directing substantial effort at lobbying the few senators whose votes were likely to prove decisive.

Following up on evidence corroborating the proposed strategies of presidential influence, I then take up the important question of their effectiveness – in other words, whether they work. To investigate the answer, I started by drawing from the Policy Agendas Project (www.policyagendas.org) comprehensive taxonomy from the *Congressional Quarterly (CQ) Almanac*. Focusing this study on seven major domestic-policy domains – civil rights, community and housing, education, energy, health, social welfare, and taxes – and 55 corresponding subtopics for every Congress between the 83rd (1953–54) and the 108th (2003–4), a comprehensive survey of the Policy Agendas' dataset identified 769 relevant policy initiatives.[14] For each, a research team coded (1) the White House's involvement, and (2) the overall outcome, along with numerous other variables. We then went back and integrated data on corresponding *CQ* "key votes" for each chamber. The upshot: the dataset gathered to test the effectiveness of presidents' lobbying includes 769 major domestic legislative initiatives, 113 key House votes, 100 key Senate votes for a period spanning 1953–2004: one that covers 52 years, 10 presidents, and 26 Congresses. These data offer novel measures of presidential lobbying and presidential success

---

[14] The Appendix lists the specific Policy Agendas issues and codes used in this study. The Policy Agendas team categorized initiatives into the relevant issue area up to the 107th Congress (2001–2), which I updated to include the 108th (2003–4).

(using both roll-call and non-roll-call measures), thereby affording an unprecedented examination of the relationship between the two. To this end, Chapter 4 tests presidents' success in *CQ*'s key votes, and Chapter 5 investigates presidents' success in the overall legislative outcome – that is, whether or not it ended with a new law in the president's preferred direction.

To conclude, Chapter 6 considers this study's broader implications for understanding and assessing presidents' role in U.S. lawmaking. Casting aside all-too-familiar "great man" theories, I offer a more modest take on presidential leadership, one that highlights the principled and pragmatic decisions all presidents must make given the resources they can control and the constraints they cannot. So although I do not offer any simple answers as to what "real" leadership entails, I do set forth the trade-offs that real leaders must weigh. In doing so, the concluding chapter pulls the book's theoretical threads to uncover the normative implications for citizens, scholars, and presidents alike.

CHAPTER TWO

A Theory of Positive Presidential Power

Opportunities to host landmark signing ceremonies are highly prized inside the White House. Such auspicious occasions allow the president not just to help chart the nation's course against the day's most pressing problems but also to bask in the flattering glow of political achievement. And given the myriad of challenges the legislative process presents, perhaps it is forgivable that when Congress has passed their signature policy initiatives, one president after another has employed far more pageantry than required by the Constitution's modest demand that "he shall sign it." After all, what president could pass up moments like these?

- On a beautiful summer day in Harry Truman's hometown of Independence, Missouri, with Harry Truman at his side, President Lyndon Johnson signed into law Medicare, the historic health-care program Mr. Truman had first proposed more than a decade earlier. Introducing President Johnson, Truman declared: "Mr. President, I am glad to have lived this long and to witness today the signing of the Medicare bill which puts this Nation right where it needs to be, to be right. Your inspired leadership and a responsive forward-looking Congress have made it historically possible for this day to come about. Thank all of you most highly for coming here. It is an honor I haven't had for, well, quite awhile, I'll say that to you, but here it is: Ladies and gentlemen, the President of the United States" (30 July 1965).
- Atop the hills of Santa Barbara, California, as President Reagan signed the Economic Recovery Tax Act of 1981, his sunny mood

cut through the foggy air. Sitting alone before assembled reporters (and not flanked by the usual array of congressional and administrative officials), the president joked about the weather, the press, and the number of pens laid out for his use. But most of all, Reagan celebrated the legislative change he had called for and helped bring about. Just before signing the legislation, he declared the moment as signaling "an end to the excessive growth in government bureaucracy, government spending, government taxing" (13 August 1981).

- Days before he signed it into law, President Bill Clinton's budget package and top domestic priority passed Congress by the narrowest possible margin, with the last tie-breaking vote being cast by Vice President Al Gore. At the signing ceremony, President Clinton acknowledged, "This was clearly not an easy fight" but emphasized that the achievement justified the effort (10 August 1993). It was a point the president reasserted years later, when commemorating the law's fifth anniversary. He noted, "All of you know that it's one of those rare moments, as the Vice President said, where you can literally say that this has happened because of the energy and spirit of the American people, but also because we passed an economic plan that liberated that energy and spirit" (23 April 1998).

- Undaunted by the day's freezing temperatures, Ohioans waiting to see President George W. Bush sign the nation's new education law cheered as *Marine One* reached Hamilton High School. Later, inside the gymnasium, the president returned the favor: "I want to thank all who've come to witness this historic moment. . . . Most bills are signed at the White House, but I decided to sign this bill in one of the most important places in America: a public school." Reflecting on the law's broader significance, Mr. Bush called it "a great symbol of what is possible in Washington when good people come together to do what's right." (8 January 2002)

However intensely presidents may aspire to legislative triumphs like those of Johnson, Reagan, Clinton, and Bush, the strategic roadmap from proposal to passage remains obscure. The ends are obvious; the means are not. When running through Capitol Hill's intricate gauntlet of different chambers, committees, and parties; leaders and caucuses;

rules and folkways – not to mention 535 independent legislators – each with his or her own incentives and interests, how can presidents best build winning coalitions for their policies? What's more, how should the president tailor his coalition-building strategies to fit his particular moment – the Congress he confronts and the political muscle he brandishes (or doesn't)?

At first blush, searching for systematic strategies behind presidents' legislative influence may seem a fool's errand. After all, even those close to its workings often seem perplexed by the capitol's policymaking practices. *The Hill,* a Washington newspaper that specializes in congressional news, describes its mission as reporting "the inner workings of Congress, the pressures confronting policy makers and the many ways – often unpredictable – in which decisions are made." It is this seemingly erratic character that has led many a scholar and practitioner to infer that each president's legislative challenge is unique, distinctive to a particular time and the particular people who happen to occupy it.

Acknowledging the complexities, there remain compelling reasons to think that a parsimonious, portable theory of presidents' positive power in Congress exists. The heart of Washington's legislative process – where the stakes are high, the rules of the game are (relatively) clear, and the players are highly informed – renders presidential-congressional relations an area ripe for social-scientific theorizing (see esp. Cameron 2000, chap. 3). Inasmuch as players have both the incentive and the information they need to best utilize whatever hand they are dealt, *if* we can distill the policymaking game to its essential elements, *then* we can uncover players' incentives, foresee their choices, and predict the results.[1] This, I argue, is precisely the opportunity presented by presidential-congressional interactions regarding important domestic legislation. This chapter explains why.

---

[1] Morris Fiorina (1974, 29) described the theorist's assignment well: "Like all theoretical worlds, the one we posit is more or less unrealistic, an idealization of the empirical reality we hope to explain. But if we abstract appropriately and capture the most important features of the empirical situation, then we may expect to find that the theoretical processes present in the model world bear some correspondence to the behavior we observe in the empirical world."

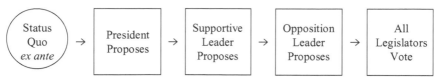

Figure 2.1 A Model of Lawmaking.

2.1   THE BASIC POLICYMAKING GAME

In contrast to the practical reality that Congress has enough employees and organizational components to fill an almanac – literally – its analytical core is fairly straightforward: picking a preferred policy among rival alternatives. To clarify presidents' proactive policymaking role, then, let me begin by making a few simplifying assumptions about presidents, lawmakers, and the lawmaking process. Specifically, let me introduce the theory as a game among three players – the president, a supportive leader, and an opposing leader – who propose policies to appeal to a fourth and final player: the pivotal voter.[2] Figure 2.1 illustrates this policymaking game.

As depicted in the figure, the basic legislative model utilized here envisions that the president and congressional leaders play a key role in setting Congress' agenda, while swing voters play a decisive role later on.[3] More precisely, the president kicks off the process by proposing to replace some status quo policy with one of his own, at which point his side's congressional leader may either affirm the president's proposal or introduce an independent one.[4] With the president and his supportive leader's proposal on the board, the opposition leader can then offer a different proposal. The basic game concludes when all lawmakers vote between rival alternatives, with the pivotal voter's choice determining the outcome.

---

[2] Put differently, the president and each side's congressional leaders propose policies to satisfy their preferences *and* win on the floor.

[3] In partitioning the legislative earlygame from its endgame, I fully endorse Cox and McCubbins' (2005) assessment that "there is a substantial empirical payoff to separating the agenda-setting and voting stages of the legislative process" (49).

[4] The president and his party leaders ultimately offer just one proposal. However, because each *can* propose an independent bill, the president and his party's congressional leaders have to work out whose preferences, exactly, are reflected in that proposal.

To explicate the game and its implications more fully, let me take up its constituent stages, working backward from endgame to earlygame. I follow up that analysis by examining how various complications, such as closed voting rules and unified versus divided government, affect the basic model.

2.1.1   The Legislative Endgame (Voting)

Few skills are as highly prized inside the Beltway as those in "the arcane art and mystical science of counting votes," as *The New York Times* called it (19 November 2006). In fact, so-called nose counts, head counts, or whip counts have currency precisely because floor votes ultimately decide legislative debates and members often hedge (and occasionally dissemble) about their preferences before these votes. When President George W. Bush's team prevailed in a close, controversial trade vote, the president publicly commended a key legislative ally for accurately forecasting the outcome: "I want to thank my fellow Texan, Tom DeLay, the best vote-counter in the history of the United States Congress [laughter and applause]" (6 August 2002).

To be sure, practitioners are not the only ones to recognize the crucial role of floor votes in congressional lawmaking. Actually, researchers have done far more than highlight roll-call votes' importance; they have explored the implications. Duncan Black's (1948) and Anthony Downs's (1957) pioneering works showed that even when votes are distributed equally – that is, one member, one vote – only certain members will decide the outcome. Specifically, Black and Downs each proved that if legislators are aligned ideologically and an issue is decided by majority rule, the group's median voter will pick what (or who) wins.[5] More recent work has built on this foundation to incorporate important supermajoritarian voting rules: the three-fifths vote needed for cloture in the Senate and the two-thirds vote needed to override a presidential veto in both chambers (see Brady and Volden 1998; Krehbiel 1998).

---

[5] Importantly, Poole and Rosenthal's (1997) work analyzing lawmakers' preferences shows that congressional voting comports well with the argument that members typically vote according to their ideology, organized along a single dimension, liberal to conservative. So the one-dimensional policy space is theoretically critical (see Arrow 1951; Grofman 2004; McKelvey 1976) and generally empirically appropriate.

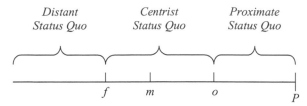

Figure 2.2 Implications of the Legislative Endgame.

Figure 2.2 illustrates the pivotal voters whose preferences reign supreme for different voting rules when members have symmetrical preferences and a conservative president, P, is in office. As the figure shows, the pivotal voter in any given case depends on the location of the status quo and the voting rule needed to replace it. Status quos proximate to the president's position invoke one set of rules (related to the presidential veto); status quos distant from the president's position invoke a different set (related to nonveto passage). Although this study focuses on the latter cases – that is, those where the president seeks to replace some distant status quo policy with one closer to his own preference – let me briefly examine both situations.

The first class of presidential–congressional interactions is also the one most rigorously studied: veto bargaining (see Cameron 2000; Kiewit and McCubbins 1988). Here, the president prefers a proximate status quo – that is, one on his preferred side of the pivotal voter – to a new policy proposal and, as such, strategically uses his veto power to blunt, if not outright kill, the proposed change. Because the Constitution requires two-thirds agreement of each house to override the president's veto, the "pivotal voter" who ultimately determines the outcome is each chamber's 34th percentile member (the 34th senator and the 146th representative closest to the president). By retaining the decisive position on veto-override votes, these so-called override pivots, o, determine whether the president's veto is sustained or overriden.

In contrast to veto-bargaining situations (where the president prefers the status quo to some proposed rival) are issues on which the president dislikes a far-off status quo and wants to replace it with a bill better reflecting his preference. Now the pivotal voter who decides the president's fate depends on the chamber. Under the simple majority rule that governs the House of Representatives, it is the median voter,

m, who controls the outcome; under the three-fifths supermajority rule that typically rules the Senate, the decisive vote sits with the sixtieth member opposite the president's side, f.[6]

One obvious point deserves emphasis: although the general rules that define pivotal voters – the override pivots, as well as the House median voter and Senate filibuster pivot – are applicable to any Congress, their actual manifestations will vary dramatically from Congress to Congress. Using Poole and Rosenthal's DW-NOMINATE estimates of lawmakers' ideological predispositions (based on their roll-call voting patterns), Table 2.1 reports the ideological distance between Congress' pivotal voters and postwar presidents' ideological side, scaled from 0 to 2.[7] As the table reports, some presidents have enjoyed pivotal voters relatively close to their preferred position (e.g., President Carter in 1977), while others have confronted Congresses with pivotal voters clearly predisposed to opposing them (e.g., President Ford in 1975).

Also noteworthy is that the same president often faces dramatically different pivotal voters at different points during his tenure. Take President Dwight Eisenhower, for example. While the number of voters Eisenhower needed to win over remained the same in the Eighty-Third (1953–54) and Eighty-Sixth (1959–60) Congresses, the ideological predispositions of the senators who held those votes were markedly different. Figure 2.3 illustrates how much more amenable the filibuster pivot of Eisenhower's first year was compared to the one during his final year.

In sum, a rich literature has uncovered whose votes will ultimately decide the president's congressional fortunes when promoting his legislative initiatives: the House's median voter and the Senate's filibuster pivot. In the theory at the heart of this book, then, I build on this work

---

[6] Although final passage in the U.S. Senate is decided by simple majority rule, the upper chamber famously imposes an extra hurdle before debate on/obstruction of a bill can end and vote on the bill's final passage can proceed. Invoking so-called cloture required a two-thirds supermajority before 1975 and has required a sixty-vote supermajority since then.

[7] Again, because this book's goal is explaining *positive* presidential power (i.e., cases where presidents seek to change distant status quos), the pertinent pivotal voters are those crucial to passing or defeating presidential initiatives: the House's median voter and the Senate's filibuster pivot.

TABLE 2.1. *Congressional pivotal voters' distance from the president,*
1953–2004

| President | Congress (years) | Pivotal voter's distance from president[a] | |
		House (median)	Senate (filibuster pivot)
Eisenhower	83rd (1953–54)	0.88	1.04
Eisenhower	84th (1955–56)	0.95	1.19
Eisenhower	85th (1957–58)	0.95	1.18
Eisenhower	86th (1959–60)	1.07	1.31
Kennedy	87th (1961–62)	1.00	1.16
Kennedy/Johnson	88th (1963–64)	1.00	1.08
Johnson	89th (1965–66)	0.85	1.09
Johnson	90th (1967–68)	1.01	1.08
Nixon	91st (1969–70)	1.00	1.31
Nixon	92nd (1971–72)	1.04	1.27
Nixon/Ford	93rd (1973–74)	1.04	1.34
Ford	94th (1975–76)	1.19	1.35
Carter	95th (1977–78)	0.83	0.93
Carter	96th (1979–80)	0.86	0.95
Reagan	97th (1981–82)	1.05	1.13
Reagan	98th (1983–84)	1.12	1.15
Reagan	99th (1985–86)	1.10	1.16
Reagan	100th (1987–88)	1.11	1.23
Bush (41)	101st (1989–90)	1.12	1.25
Bush (41)	102nd (1991–92)	1.14	1.26
Clinton	103rd (1993–94)	0.85	1.00
Clinton	104th (1995–96)	1.19	1.25
Clinton	105th (1997–98)	1.18	1.29
Clinton	106th (1999–2000)	1.16	1.29
Bush (43)	107th (2001–2)	0.82	1.30
Bush (43)	108th (2002–4)	0.76	1.27

[a] Ideological distance scaled from 0 to 2, based on estimates from all members' roll-call voting behavior (see Poole and Rosenthal 1997).

to highlight the legislative endgame's importance and these pivotal voters' crucial role therein. In fact, the rest of the model examines how Washington's key players – both presidents and congressional leaders – try to win over these pivotal voters with their proposals and their lobbying. Let me now turn to examining these leading legislative players and their options for attracting each chamber's swing voters.

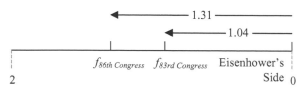

Figure 2.3 Filibuster Pivots in the Eighty-Third (1953–54) and Eighty-Sixth (1959–60) Congresses.

2.1.2 The Legislative Earlygame (Agenda Setting)

Considering pivotal voters' strategic importance in the decisive stages of U.S. lawmaking, there is a tendency to envision those wielding the capitol's crucial votes as omnipotent. In reality, pivotal voters, like all congressional members, are spread exceedingly thin. The range of substantive issues meriting their attention is staggering, and each implicates a complicated mix of members' programmatic, electoral, partisan, and personal goals. Accordingly, the problem facing swing voters and nonswing voters alike is the proverbial problem of drinking from a fire hose; there is simply too much to engage comprehensively or, often, more than tangentially.

Faced with this decision-making dilemma – too much to tackle, too little to tackle it with – lawmakers must triage. They focus on priorities and satisfice elsewhere. In practice, this means that most members only seriously engage an issue when it reaches the floor, and sometimes not even then. John Kingdon's (1989) classic study of congressional voting encapsulated members' predicament:

> In order to consider a given vote thoroughly, the congressman would need to begin his search some time ahead. But at that point, he does not know the dimensions of the issue that will finally be presented to him for decision, or even whether it will come up at all. Thus, seeing that his valuable time might very well be wasted, he does not begin considering a search until it is too late to do it at all extensively or thoroughly. (229)

Kingdon's insight squares nicely with Richard Hall's in-depth study of congressmen's legislative participation. Hall showed how resource constraints – time, energy, staff, and so on – force most members to "rationally abdicate" substantial amounts of legislative work to their colleagues. In fact, he found that only a select few played a "major role" for any given issue, much less served as a "principal author"; most members' input was "negligible" (Hall 1996, chap. 2; see also Arnold 1990; Evans 1991; Wawro 2001).

If most lawmakers do not develop, propose, and promote their own preferred policies on the day's major issues, the follow-up question is obvious: Who does? That is, who are these few policymakers who serve as "principal authors" (using Hall's label) and set the "dimensions of the issue" (in Kingdon's terms)? According to these and other researchers, the answer tends to be presidents and congressional leaders. In the model being developed here, I build on this work by incorporating presidents and leaders into the legislative earlygame, recognizing that they exercise this role with one eye on the legislative endgame.

2.1.2.1 *The president's proposal.* Amid a myriad of controversies regarding the nature and extent of presidential power, one claim goes unquestioned: the presidency gives its occupants an unequaled ability to develop and publicize policy initiatives – in other words, to help set the national policy agenda. George Edwards III and Andrew Barrett (2000), based on a detailed study of presidential agenda setting in Congress, concluded simply, "*The results are clear: the president can almost always place potentially significant legislation on the agenda of Congress*" (120; emphasis in original).[8] Jon Bond and Richard Fleisher (1990) asserted further: "The president's greatest influence over policy comes from the agenda he pursues and the way it is packaged" (220).

In the model proposed here, I acknowledge presidents' key agenda-setting role by permitting the president to submit proposals for members' consideration. In doing so, I make two assumptions about how presidents exercise this agenda-setting option. First, I assume that White House officials target "distant" status quos for change – that is, presidential initiatives attempt to replace status quo policies on the opposite side of the House median voter and Senate filibuster pivot

---

[8] Edwards and Barrett's (2000) findings are complemented by Cox and McCubbins' (2005). Of the cases where the House majority party's median member was "rolled" – i.e., was on the losing side of a vote – virtually all were in the president's preferred direction.

($sq < f$ or $m < P$). The idea here is simple: the policies presidents most want to replace are the ones with which they most disagree (see Light 1999).

Second, I make an assumption relevant to presidents' power to propose legislation that has to do with strategy. Specifically, I assume that presidents strategically adapt each proposal to facilitate its passage, a practice Larry Evans (1991) called "prior accommodation" and "greasing the skids" in the context of committee leaders. Part of this strategic anticipation is, of course, envisioning the legislative endgame described earlier. Another part of greasing the skids, although less obvious, is no less important; it involves gaming out how congressional leaders – on each side of the aisle – will react. In the following, I reveal how presidents can anticipate these leaders' actions by explaining their options and the choice among them.

2.1.2.2 The supportive leader's proposal. The interactions between presidents and their own party's congressional leadership comprise one of the more interesting (and understudied) relationships in American politics. Because presidents and their party's congressional leaders generally share a comparable ideological outlook, disagreements between the two seem anomalous. So despite infamous cases to the contrary – for example, President Carter's plan to reinvent government, President Reagan's push to legalize immigrants, and President Clinton's health-care program – the fact of the matter is that presidents and their party's leaders often find that consensus comes effortlessly. But, as I say, not always.

As a first step to seeing when presidents and their congressional leaders will work hand-in-glove and when they will be at cross-purposes, Figure 2.4 illustrates the policies with the potential to pass in a chamber (see Romer and Rosenthal 1978). That is, it indicates (by the shaded region) those policy proposals the pivotal voter would support over various status quos, which run from the status quo (sq) on one side of the pivotal voter to its transpose position on the opposite side ($-sq$). For my purposes, the critical insight is that this range of *potentially* passable policies can vary dramatically: sometimes reaching close to the president's ideal (as in Fig. 2.4a), sometimes not (as in Fig. 2.4c).

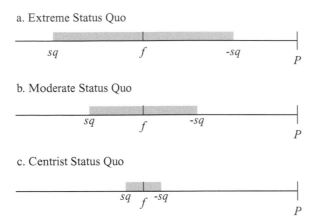

a. Extreme Status Quo

b. Moderate Status Quo

c. Centrist Status Quo

Figure 2.4 Range of Potentially Passable Policies for Different Status Quos: (a) Extreme, (b) Moderate, and (c) Centrist.

Now incorporating a president's own congressional leaders into this mix, as in Figure 2.5, we can see when any policy "daylight" between the president and his leading allies can complicate matters and when it will not. To this end, let us imagine two congressional leaders – one centrist (S_c), one extremist (S_e) – who share the president's basic ideology (conservative) but diverge to differing degrees, the centrist more than the extremist.

In the case of an extreme president with an extreme congressional leader, neither has the *potential* to pass his or her ideal bill ($-sq < S < P$). As such, whatever disagreements they may have are not relevant; both now want to pass a bill as close to $-sq$ as possible. More generally, whenever the president and supportive congressional leaders hold similar preferences, at least among the range of policies that can potentially pass, agreement over what policy to propose arrives naturally.[9] In fact, here the president's and his congressional leaders' principal challenge is not forging agreement on legislative substance but rather coordinating efforts on legislative strategy. Such is why Steven Smith (2007) says, "As a practical matter, a president and party leaders of the president's party are likely to seek to influence legislative

[9] This may overstate intraparty harmony a bit. In practice, presidents and supportive leaders care about their proposals qua proposals, so sincere preferences can create conflicts early, even if those differences are unlikely to be relevant as the process goes forward.

Figure 2.5 Presidents' and Supportive Leaders' Preferences.

outcomes in mutually compatible ways and, typically, with an explicit sense of teamwork" (72).

In contrast, tensions can arise when the president engages a more centrist congressional leader ($S < -sq < P$). Here, the congressional leader has the incentive to advocate an individual preference, S_c, rather than one closer to the president (say, $-sq$), as undercutting the president's proposal with his or her own helps this centrist leader to ensure that Congress passes legislation better reflecting his or her policy beliefs. So unless the president's congressional leaders are willing to subjugate their own interests to "carry the president's water," intraparty negotiations may be required to reach agreement about what policy, exactly, they will propose and promote.[10]

That being said, there is one thing that can convince presidents and their congressional leaders to overlook any internal disagreements: the opposition. When challenged by a strong, strategic opposing leader, the range of potentially passable policies constricts, potentially obviating the significance of whatever intramural disputes might otherwise divide the president from his supporting leaders. Let us now examine these opposing leaders.

2.1.2.3   *The opposing leader's proposal.* Exchanges between presidents and their leading legislative opponents are always newsworthy, occasionally legendary. Still familiar are tales from the strategic rivalries between Dwight Eisenhower and (then Senate Majority Leader) Lyndon Johnson, Bill Clinton and Newt Gingrich, and, perhaps most famously, Ronald Reagan and Tip O'Neill. Speaking of President Reagan, Speaker O'Neill remembered: "He calls up: 'Tip, you and I are political enemies only until 6 o'clock. It's 4 o'clock now. Can

---

[10] An aide to Robert Byrd (D-WV) recounted how Senator Byrd viewed his role as leader vis-à-vis his party's president differently than did Senator Howard Baker (R-TN). "Byrd used to lament that he was never Jimmy Carter's man, but the Senate's man. And he could not understand why Baker had become Reagan's man" (*Politico*, 20 November 2008).

we pretend it's 6 o'clock?' How can you dislike a guy like that?" (*Los Angeles Times*, 6 June 2004).

Given each president's ability to push a legislative agenda, out-party congressional leaders often find themselves in a reactive posture – even when they have a majority in Congress. Yet even though they cannot veto the president's initiatives, a president's leading congressional opponents enjoy a much stronger position than the "the loyal opposition" in a parliamentary system. As Richard Cohen observed (1992), "Congress provides more leverage for opponents to stop controversial bills than for supporters to pass it" (67). Beyond criticizing the president and his proposals, opposing leaders' leverage derives from a myriad of opportunities for obstructionism, not to mention their capacity to challenge the president's proposal with one of their own.

My basic legislative model reflects leading opponents' position by allowing them to counter the president's (and his supportive leaders') proposal.[11] Like presidents, I assume that opposing leaders use their agenda-setting power strategically, drafting proposals not only to satisfy their personal beliefs but also to attract the pivotal voter's support. Therefore, in cases where the president (along with his leading allies) and opposing leaders are on opposite sides of the pivotal voter ($O < f < S/P$), as is typical, the optimal strategy for an opposing leader looking to beat the president's proposal is simple: propose one closer to the pivotal voter. Even if this does not ultimately lead to the leading opponent's success, it does force the president and his allies to moderate their proposal (kicking off a process that, if unaltered by lobbying, ultimately follows a "race to the middle" – a sequential bargain to the pivotal voter's preferred position).

2.1.3 A Note on Divided Government

The basic model just developed depicts a more or less nonpartisan policymaking process. This is so because pivotal voters' influence comes from their policy preference (rather than their party affiliation), and each "side's" leaders have unfettered access to the floor

[11] I take obstructionism to be functionally equivalent to proposing the status quo.

(rather than the majority party leader having advantages vis-à-vis his or her minority party counterparts). Before turning to presidents' strategies for influencing lawmakers and legislation within this model, it is useful to consider first how empowering the majority party affects presidents' basic policymaking prospects – either for better (during unified government) or, potentially, for worse (during divided government).

2.1.3.1 *Majority party leaders: negative agenda control.* Recent research has found that the strongest roots feeding majority party power are of two sorts: negative and positive.[12] The first of these, negative power, comes primarily from majority leaders' control over the legislative calendar (see esp. Cox and McCubbins 2005). By strategically deciding what comes first, later, or not at all, the majority's party and committee leaders can put disfavored (i.e., distant) status quos up for reconsideration while keeping favored (i.e., proximate) status quos off the congressional calendar altogether. This comprises a "negative" power because its essence is not promoting preferred bills but rather blocking dispreferred policy changes. And, in terms of policy, the prediction is that nearly all legislative changes move the nation's laws away from the minority party's preference, toward the majority party's.

But in demonstrating the significance of the majority party's negative agenda power, theoretically and empirically, Cox and McCubbins (2005) further point out its primary limitation: the president. They say: "Plausibly, presidents can focus public attention on issues of their own choosing, thereby pressuring an otherwise reluctant House majority to take action.... [If so,] the majority may sometimes be forced into a more or less straightforward final-passage vote on an issue not of their choosing and be rolled as a consequence" (119). Regarding the majority's negative agenda power, then, the basic picture that emerges is one where majority party leaders can generally block minority party leaders' legislative agenda but not the president's (see also Mayhew 2005).

---

[12] As noted earlier, many have detailed how members' overwhelming workload demands that they delegate some decision making to their colleagues, especially their leaders (see Arnold 1990; Hall 1996; Kingdon 1989; Krehbiel 1991). Inasmuch as it is possible, members abdicate this authority to leaders who will protect their party's reputation (Cox and McCubbins 1993, 2005) and serve their policy goals (Aldrich and Rohde 2001; Rohde 1991; Van Houweling 2009).

As suggestive as their results may be, it is important to note that Cox and McCubbins do not identify *how* presidents exert influence in Congress; the paths of positive presidential power remain in the proverbial "black box." By delineating the causal mechanisms behind presidents' legislative influence, then, the basic model developed throughout this chapter fills in what cartel theory leaves out – that is, cases of major domestic issues where the president proposes and promotes his preferred outcome. Considering that this includes most of the postwar era's most important, controversial legislative debates, explicating presidents' proactive role therein thus offers important insights on partisan cartels, presidential power, and the relationship between the two. Indeed, we are able to see why a president can cement the majority party's negative agenda control during unified government and "roll" it during divided government.

2.1.3.2 Majority party leaders: positive agenda control. If the majority party's foremost grip on congressional power comes from negative agenda control, the second source, less firmly held, comes from positive agenda control (see Aldrich 1995; Aldrich and Rhode 2001; Campbell, Cox, and McCubbins 2002; Cox and McCubbins 1993, 2005; Evans 1991; Rohde 1991; Sinclair 1983, 1995; Smith 1989, 2007).[13] Per this option, majority party leaders go beyond censoring the status quos subject to debate; they further censor minority party leaders' ability to propose their own bills. So here, majority party leaders get exclusive authority to pick which policy among the *potentially* passable ones actually does pass (see Fig. 2.4 and preceding discussion). Not surprisingly, presidents under unified government benefit if the majority party's leaders exert positive agenda control; however, more surprisingly, under divided government, the president *does not* suffer even if majority party leaders generally enjoy positive agenda control in Congress. Let me explain.

Figure 2.6 amends my basic policymaking model to grant majority party leaders positive agenda power under unified government

---

[13] Cox and McCubbins (2005) emphasize the asymmetries between the majority party's two power options, negative and positive agenda control, with the former being much more robust than the latter. They cite negative agenda control as "the bedrock of party government" and positive agenda control as its "superstructure."

a. Unified Government

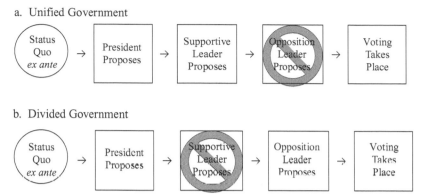

b. Divided Government

Figure 2.6 The Basic Policymaking Game under Unified (a) and Divided (b) Government (with Closed Rules).

(Fig. 2.6a) and divided government (Fig. 2.6b). Naturally, the unified government situation largely dovetails the basic positive agenda control described previously; the only difference is that the president also gets to propose an alternative. Because presidents and their leaders will typically have comparable preferences over passable alternatives (see sect. 2.1.2.2), they will also exercise their party's positive agenda power similarly. In cases where the president and a congressional leader disagree, the more moderate of the two is best positioned to prevail (absent any lobbying).

More interesting, therefore, are positive agenda control's implications under divided government, as in Figure 2.6b. Here, we see that even when opposing leaders restrict the president's leading allies' access to the floor, unless they can also block the president's proposals (which, in the previous section, I argued they cannot), then congressional lawmaking effectively mirrors the nonpartisan model I consider. Indeed, we end up with a game between two players – the president and an opposing leader – who compete for a third player's (the pivotal legislator's) vote. This is comparable to the basic policymaking model already presented but without the supportive leader's being able to undercut the president. And that potential, I have already shown, is rarely relevant when the president faces a strong, strategic opposing leader, as he does under divided government.

In sum, presidents' unique capacity to get their initiatives onto the legislative calendar disrupts typical partisan patterns in Congress.

With unified government, the president buttresses his agenda-setting options with those of his leading allies; both work together to change the same "distant" status quos and protect the same "proximate" ones. These efforts are streamlined if Congress' party leaders exercise negative agenda control and cemented further if they enjoy positive agenda control. With divided government, by contrast, the president's ability to circumvent the majority leaders' agenda-setting barriers, negative or positive, reduces the importance of partisanship per se and elevates the importance of preferences, especially those of the pivotal voters.

Accordingly, this logic suggests that presidents' potential influence increases under unified government and *does not* decrease under divided government, at least for initiatives on which the president invests time, energy, and other resources advocating on Capitol Hill.[14] Assuming a nonpartisan policymaking process, as I do, thus offers a conservative appraisal of presidents' prospects for legislative leadership.

2.2   THE STRATEGIES OF PRESIDENTIAL INFLUENCE

In the stylized legislature developed to this point, policymaking proceeds across two basic stages: an earlygame, in which the president and congressional leaders offer policy proposals, followed by an endgame, where pivotal voters decide which alternative prevails. So far, however, only the endgame stage has affected the outcome. As we have seen, in angling to attract the requisite number of votes, the president and congressional leaders have engaged in a "race to the middle" that ends only when they accede to the pivotal voter's policy wishes.

But the legislative environment in which pivotal voters' reign has emerged is a rather sterile one. It confines members' interests to the policy issue at hand, treats their preferences on that issue as fixed, and assumes that each player's only course of action is passively

---

[14] It is worth reiterating that when a president chooses to ignore an issue, the majority party's singular importance resurfaces. Indeed, as Cox and McCubbins (2005) convincingly show, absent White House involvement, the House's policymaking channels will almost always flow in the majority's preferred direction – toward the president during unified government, away during divided government.

endorsing his or her preferences. There is no room for arm-twisting, for browbeating, for deal making.

The real world of Washington politics is decidedly less antiseptic. For one thing, lawmakers care about more than one policy topic at a time, as well as a myriad of nonlegislative matters. In the most famous formulations, Richard Fenno (1978) and John Kingdon (1989) identify legislators' three basic goals: winning reelection, passing "good" policy, and increasing their influence within Congress (see also Fiorina 1974). So, far from being single-minded, single-issue advocates, members also value things like attracting media attention, attending public rallies, raising campaign funds, affecting presidential appointees, revising bureaucratic rules, and so on, into the distance. And, of course, personal egos also play a role; Washington politicians care about invitations, acknowledgments, trinkets, and other matters of personal importance.

Because legislative issues implicate a variety of goals and members do not consider policy questions in a vacuum, policymakers' preferences are neither preset nor preordained. Changing the programmatic or electoral incentives an issue evokes is likely to change a lawmaker's position on that issue. And while most lawmakers' goals harmoniously align on any given policy question, sometimes they do not (see Conley and Yon 2007; Covington 1988; Kingdon 1989; Sullivan 1987, 1990).

To whatever extent legislators' preferences and the policymaking process are in fact malleable, that White House officials actively seek to bend both to the president's advantage is hardly surprising. After all, from the administration's point of view, better than tailoring the president's proposal to fit congressional realities is the opposite: manipulating congressional realities to accommodate the president's proposals.

Figure 2.7 adds presidents' informal lobbying to the basic policymaking game. Now, rather than just being able to propose legislation in light of leaders' proposals and pivotal voters' preferences, the White House can actually seek to influence those lawmakers, their preferences, and their votes. In fact, we can now see inside presidents' strategic playbook: beyond their unique ability to propel initiatives onto the legislative agenda, modern chief executives can further promote their proposals by *shifting the distribution of preferences* on

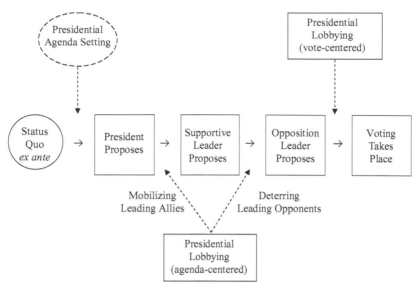

Figure 2.7 A Model of Lawmaking with Presidential Lobbying.

roll-call votes and by *censoring the policy alternatives* that make it that far. The first of these constitutes a vote-centered strategy; the second, an agenda-centered strategy. Let me explain each, again starting with the endgame and working backward to the earlygame.

2.2.1   The Endgame Strategy (Vote-Centered Lobbying)

Washington folklore is replete with tales of presidents' tactical maneuvering just before crucial roll-call votes. A *New York Times Magazine* story, entitled "Taking Charge of Congress" (9 August 1981), contemporaneously reported one that has been frequently recounted since:

> It had been raining most of the morning two Sundays ago when President Reagan came out of his personal lodge at the Presidential hideaway in the Catoctin Mountains to greet 15 Democratic Congressmen. He had invited them up for lunch and a bit of lobbying.... For half an hour they all swapped small talk over coffee, orange juice, and Bloody Marys on the flagstone patio overlooking a rustic country-club setting of terraced gardens, a swimming pool and nearby woods.... After lunch, President Reagan stood up. 'Now for the commercial,' he smiled, launching into a brief pitch for his three-year tax-cut package which was due for a showdown vote in the House of Representatives three days hence.

Certainly, President Reagan's lobbying efforts are hardly peculiar; comparable vote-seeking activities are in all modern presidents' persuasive repertoire. Lyndon Johnson called Abe Ribicoff (D-CT) about his tax bill to say, "Goddamn it, you need to vote with me once in a while – just one time" (Miller Center of Public Affairs 2000, 26); Jimmy Carter reportedly "made improper political trade-offs to win the votes of crucial senators" for important provisions in his energy bill (*Congressional Quarterly* [*CQ*] *Almanac* 1978, 659); and George W. Bush's play for votes on a trade bill "resembled the wheeling and dealing on a car lot" (*The Washington Post*, 28 July 2005). But perhaps the most memorable exchanges of this sort occurred when Bill Clinton, trying to scrape together enough "ayes" to pass his deficit reduction package, frantically sought to win Senator Bob Kerrey's (D-NE) decisive vote (see Stephanopoulos 1999). OMB Director Leon Panetta described the scene:

> We're getting close to the vote. We're trying to locate Kerrey. And somebody tells us that he's in a movie theater in downtown Washington someplace. And we're all going nuts, saying, 'What the hell is he doing going to the show when we got this big vote coming up tomorrow?' And so we even went as far as to try to find out, well, what theater is he in? Where is he? Can we try to get him? (*Frontline: The Clinton Years*, 2001)

Although they ultimately decided against interrupting Senator Kerrey's screening, the president's Legislative Affairs team did set up a meeting between Kerrey and President Clinton first thing the next morning, which they followed with several more calls from various staffers as well as the president himself. Mr. Kerrey ultimately relented, and at a commemorative event years later, President Clinton recalled their exchanges, joking, "I would like to thank especially Bob Kerrey for never releasing the contents of our last telephone conversation. [Laughter]" (23 April 1998).

2.2.1.1   The logic of vote-centered lobbying. To political scientists, these anecdotes and the scores like them are unsurprising. As noted, presidential and congressional scholars alike have cited the paramount importance of roll-call votes and, in turn, found that forging a

winning voting coalition necessarily resides at the heart of any White
House lobbying offensive. King (1983) explains, "All you [the pres-
ident] really need from Congress is votes, but you need those votes
very badly" (247); Bond and Fleisher (1990) add, "Votes, therefore,
are the basic commodity of presidential-congressional relations" (8);
and Edwards (1989) asserts, "Presidential leadership of Congress typically revolves around obtaining or maintaining support for the chief
executive's legislative stances" (4).

In preparation for a floor fight just before voting takes place, as with
presidents' vote-centered lobbying in Figure 2.7, presidents ought not
target all members, as we have seen (see esp. Groseclose and Snyder
1996; Snyder 1991). White House officials can ignore some lawmakers
because there is little chance that they will support the president; others, because there is little chance that they will oppose him. Between
these unwavering opponents and steadfast allies are Congress' swing
voters – the members near decisive "pivot points," given the chamber's
preference distribution (see esp. Brady and Volden 1998; Krehbiel
1998). These are the pivotal voters who will ultimately decide whether
the president secures the requisite support of 218 representatives and
60 senators; therefore, the first option for an administration looking
to pass a presidential initiative is clear: *lobby the pivotal voters.*

Figure 2.8 illustrates the logic of the White House's vote-centered
strategy. Here, using whatever political capital (C_p) he possesses, the
president first targets the pivotal voter (f), and then, as f moves
toward the president's position, the interval of lawmakers between
that pivotal voter's predisposition and some point closer to the

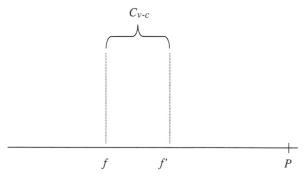

Figure 2.8 Vote-Centered Lobbying.

president's position (f to f') (see esp. Snyder 1991). Notice that although this lobbying may take any number of tactical forms – from personal appeals (e.g., Neustadt 1990[1960]) to public browbeating (e.g., Canes-Wrone 2001; Kernell 1993) to cashing in on "options" from previous interactions (e.g., King and Zeckhauser 2003) – the logic motivating this basic vote-centered strategy remains the same: shifting lawmakers' distribution of preferences to minimize the distance between the pivotal voter's position and the president's ideal.

2.2.1.2 The consequences of vote-centered lobbying. In looking at the logic motivating presidents' endgame strategy, it is easy to see what determines its effectiveness. Given a particular preference distribution and pivotal voter, the president's influence from vote-centered lobbying depends on (1) the political capital he spends, and (2) members' responsiveness to that expenditure.

Figure 2.9 translates the president's vote-centered strategy into its influence over the policy outcome. To help illustrate the findings, I rotate the standard left–right ideological spectrum counterclockwise by ninety degrees, yielding a vertical axis of policy content that runs conservative to liberal, top to bottom. On the horizontal axis is the political capital the president invests in promoting this particular policy initiative, from none on the left to some theoretical maximum

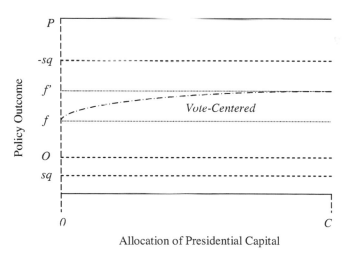

Figure 2.9 Presidential Influence via Vote-Centered Lobbying.

on the right. Finally, I consider lawmakers of two types – "pliant" and "resilient" – to capture the idea that sometimes members are more responsive to presidential appeals than others.

As Figure 2.9 shows, presidents' vote-centered lobbying activities always improve their legislative prospects. Even modest allocations of political capital can pull the outcome from the pivotal voter's pre-disposition, f, to some point closer to the president's. Obviously, the more capital the president spends, the more influence he exerts. So too when lawmakers are members who are especially responsive to presidential arm-twisting and deal making. However, one final point revealed by Figure 2.9 is less obvious but no less important: presidents see decreasing policy returns on each additional unit of political cap-ital allocated to vote-centered lobbying. This diminishing marginal return on investment occurs because the president must induce more and more pivotal voters to move as they approach the president's preferred outcome.[15]

2.2.2 The Earlygame Strategy (Agenda-Centered Lobbying)

For reporters drawn to dramatic and decisive moments, presidential–congressional negotiations occurring in the legislative earlygame can seem less "newsworthy" than those occurring later. Earlygame exchanges take place largely in private, often among surrogates, usu-ally without a firm deadline, and only occasionally with a clear res-olution. Contrasted with the intrigue and imminence of endgame lobbying, then, prevoting processes can seem pedestrian.

Although journalists' and practitioners' reports of presidential–congressional interactions oversample from the later stages, what we do know about prevoting negotiations is instructive. Take, for exam-ple, Lyndon Johnson's efforts to promote his landmark education bill, which he described in his memoirs, *The Vantage Point* (1971):

> The danger lay now with Senate amendments, which could upset the delicate balance of the bill's various provisions. I talked with Wayne Morse, the floor manager, and with other Senate leaders of both

---

[15] The marginal effectiveness of vote-centered lobbying is attenuated further if we think, as I do, that legislators require increasing amounts of political capital for each additional move away from their initially preferred policy outcome (see Beckmann and Kumar forthcoming).

parties. They agreed that no matter how much they might like to change some aspects of the House bill, the dangers of scuttling it in conference were too great to risk. (211)

The "delicate balance" between President Johnson and each party's congressional leaders held. No amendments were adopted and the bill passed by a deceptively comfortable margin, seventy-three to eighteen.

More recently, President Bill Clinton similarly engaged congressional leaders in intelligence sharing and deal seeking. In a striking memoir about his time as President Clinton's primary political advisor, Dick Morris (1998) explained how he operated a backchannel between the White House and the Senate Majority Leader, Trent Lott (R-MS), for whom Morris had previously worked: "I kept the president well informed of my dealings with Lott, and with the president's full knowledge, I kept Lott informed of the president's thinking. Clinton encouraged use of this channel" (76; see also Lott 2005, chap. 10). And the White House's interactions with Republican leaders did not end with Senator Lott. At one meeting, President Clinton's Chief of Staff, Leon Panetta, told Speaker Newt Gingrich, "I'm trying to figure out where the votes are, Newt. There's no point in cutting a deal if the votes aren't there" (Drew 1996, 308).

Perhaps more insightful than these anecdotes, though, is the aforementioned case of President Ronald Reagan's first tax cut. While remembered mostly for its endgame lobbying – including Reagan's last-minute Oval Office address, which led to a *Washington Post* article headlined, "President's Speech Has Hill Switchboard Ablaze" – it is noteworthy that the administration's ultimate focus on swing voters was not always so.

Upon first entering the White House, President Reagan's advisors set up an ad hoc group (the Legislative Strategy Group [LSG]), chaired by James Baker, to run the administration's lobbying offensive – in their words, a "full-court press." In its earliest phases, the LSG cast a wide net, with President Reagan personally meeting 467 legislators during his first 100 days in office (Cannon 2000, 90).[16] However, beyond these brief meet-and-greets was the more central part of

[16] The joke on Capitol Hill at the time was that lawmakers had seen President Reagan more often in four months than they had seen President Carter in four years.

the administration's earlygame lobbying: seeking a "deal" with Democratic leaders. Per this effort, the White House engaged these opposition leaders with a mix of friendly gestures and hard bargaining.
Examples of the former included rescheduling the president's State
of the Union address to accommodate Ways and Means Chairman Dan
Rostenkowsi (D-IL), responding to Speaker Thomas O'Neill's (D-MA)
request for the president to aide him in support of raising the debt
ceiling, and offering these opposition leaders extra tickets to a prein-
augural extravaganza attended by numerous celebrities. Intermeshed
with these softer appeals, the White House added some harder ones.
In one call to Speaker O'Neill, President Reagan began dictating his
priorities when the Speaker interrupted him, "Did you ever hear of
the separation of powers?" President Reagan tersely shot back, "I know
the Constitution," before returning to his requests. And at a speech
in Representative Rostenkowski's district, President Reagan reminded
the chairman's constituents:

> Within the last few weeks the Congress of the United States has
> been an arena of ideas and courage, where elected representa-
> tives summoned strength born not of politics, but of statesmanship.
> Led by Republicans and joined by, as I've called them, discerning
> Democrats, the Congress voted to turn away from the established
> pattern of more and more spending and bigger and bigger govern-
> ment. Men and women of both parties are coming together with a
> spirit and drive that can only mean great things for all Americans.
> (7 July 1981)

The White House's efforts to ply Democratic congressional leaders,
however, eventually subsided. The administration shifted course as
Democratic leaders, emboldened by their sense that "the political
winds might be shifting in their favor on the tax issue," became unwilling to make substantial concessions (*The Washington Post*, 26 March
1981). Recognizing opposing leaders' increasing intransigency, President Reagan called them to the White House, reportedly to tell them,
"Fellows, we want you, but if you won't come, we're going another
way." Just as Democratic leaders thought they would be able to prevail
in an endgame floor flight, so did President Reagan. According to
Treasury Secretary Donald Regan, the president was convinced that

"[undecided members] will come around to our point of view" (*The New York Times*, 30 May 1981). As we now know, the president's forecast proved prescient.

2.2.2.1 *The logic of agenda-centered lobbying.* To the cynic, meetings between White House officials and congressional leaders offer little more than pageantry – an opportunity to portray legislative work, not to do it. And, to be sure, sometimes these interbranch exchanges entail little more than pleasantries and pictures.

However, many close observers of the presidential–congressional relationship have long cited prevoting bargaining across Pennsylvania Avenue as being substantively important. For example, discussing President Eisenhower's legislative record in 1953, *CQ* staffers issued a caveat they have often repeated in the years since:

> The President's leadership often was tested beyond the glare spotlighting roll calls.... Negotiations off the floor and action in committee sometimes are as important as the recorded votes. (*CQ Almanac* 1953, 77)

Many a political scientist has agreed. Charles Jones (1994), for one, wrote, "However they are interpreted, roll call votes cannot be more than they are: one form of floor action on legislation. If analysts insist on scoring the president, concentrating on this stage of lawmaking can provide no more than a partial tally" (195). And Jon Bond and Richard Fleisher (1990) note that even if they ultimately are reflected in roll-call votes, "many important decisions in Congress are made in places other than floor votes and recorded by means other than roll calls..." (68).

Still, while citing earlygame processes as being potentially important, no one has yet shown how (or when) they are, much less integrated the earlygame and endgame within a unified framework. This is what I aim to accomplish here. Specifically, let me now uncover how, in addition to the familiar endgame lobbying option, presidents may also seek to exert influence in the legislative earlygame by implementing a two-pronged approach: mobilizing leading allies and deterring leading opponents.

2.2.2.1.1   Mobilizing leading allies. Through the basic policymaking game, I hinted that the marriage between presidents and their partisan leaders on Capitol Hill is one of mutual interest, not unflagging allegiance. Fortunately for White House officials, presidents and their leading allies will typically share a similar substantive outlook. The exceptions to this rule come when (1) the status quo is relatively distant (from the president's side and also the pivotal voter's predisposition), (2) the president's congressional leadership holds a position more moderate than his own, and (3) opposition leaders are unwilling or unable to counter the president's proposal with one of their own. Because the number of policy issues meeting each of these criteria is relatively small, more often than not the president's and his party leaders' preferences are coincident. This explains why John Kingdon (1989) found that "without explicit evidence to the contrary, congressmen assume that the party leadership of the president's party is speaking for the administration, or at least speaking in a way consistent with administration policy" (190).

That said, in cases where the president and his leading allies do disagree – if not on policy preferences, on matters like priorities or strategy – the White House must lobby their congressional leaders to ensure that they carry the president's water (rather than their own). Hence, presidents want supportive leaders to use *their* prerogatives to keep *the president's* proposed policies among those from which legislators choose.[17] Getting their leaders "onboard" with the president's preferences is the administration's first order of business, and the bargaining tactics they use for this purpose runs the spectrum, from personal appeals to public pressure to political deals.

But even upon securing their support, the White House's work with these supportive leaders is far from done. If anything, it has barely begun. Now the White House and their leading legislative allies must

---

[17] This solves one of the presidential–congressional literature's most glaring empirical puzzles; namely, that presidents and their fellow partisans so often express frustration with one another *despite near-unanimous agreement on votes.* Here we see that the friction between presidents and their congressional leaders comes from earlygame debates about what policy to bring to the floor, not endgame debates about whether they will support it once it is there.

work together to best promote their overlapping interests.[18] To this end, they should share policy information and political intelligence, not to mention the burden of putting them to good use. In short, after first bargaining over what policy they will advocate, the president and his leading allies should coordinate efforts to best execute that advocacy.

2.2.2.1.2 Deterring leading opponents. When the president and his leading allies advocate a particular policy alternative, ultimately deciding its destiny is the members' distribution of preferences in light of rival alternatives. The key variables at this point, therefore, are the preference distribution and the rival alternatives. The first of these – that is, the White House's endgame strategy of shifting members' preference distribution via vote-centered lobbying – has already been discussed, but still unexamined is the administration's strategy for affecting rival alternatives. Let me now consider this crucial component of the White House's earlygame strategy.

By way of introduction, it is worth emphasizing the president's motivation for affecting rival alternatives: beating the status quo is almost always easier than beating a strategic opponent. Accordingly, rather than just pulling pivotal voters toward the president's position (and away from opponents'), the White House may also want to cut a deal with leading opponents, getting them to "pull their punches" against the president's proposal, or at least something close to it. The obvious theoretical question begging, then, is the same one White House officials actually ponder: Why would an opposing leader ever endorse key planks of the president's legislative agenda?

Well, one way to secure leading opponents' submission is simply by fiat. If the president and his leading allies can prohibit, by rule, leading opponents from challenging their position, then the president's policy options are constrained only by the range of potentially passable

---

[18] Speaking of President Carter's relationship with the Senate Finance Committee's Democratic Chairman, one Carter aide offered a colorful analogy: "Having Russell Long on your side is kind of like running through a jungle being chained to a gorilla. Ain't nobody gonna bother you, but it's not an altogether pleasant journey" (Mann 1992, 373).

policies. But even if this brand of strategic censorship may occasionally occur via restrictive rules in the House of Representatives, it is not generally a viable strategy and certainly not a reliable one. First, the president's party is often in the congressional minority, and second, even when in the majority, the Senate does not allow the president's leading allies to impose restrictive rules on their leading opponents. Far from it.

Lacking the ability to censor leading opponents by decree, how can an administration keep leading opponents from challenging the president's initiatives? To foreshadow, the basic answer is that White House officials can deter leading opponents inasmuch as the president can convince them that the intrapolicy benefits of fighting are low and the extrapolicy costs are high. Let me elaborate.

Figure 2.10 lays out the tenets underlying the White House's options for deterring their leading opponents, adding to the now-familiar policy space a leading opponent, O, who joins the president, P, and pivotal voter, f (who can occupy any number of positions, f to f'). For the purposes of clarity, here I assume that the president and his supportive leader, S, agree on the policy and work together promoting it. Because an administration can rarely (if ever) get pivotal voters to support the president's *ideal* outcome, deterring leading opponents from challenging the president's bill (or some version of it) requires that the White House lobby more than pivotal voters; they must also target opposing leaders. The reason is that to be successful, presidential aides must convince their leading opponents that the policy loss they will suffer from "pulling their punches" is small and can be offset by

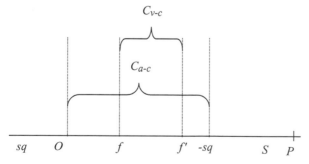

Figure 2.10 Agenda-Centered Lobbying.

gains on other fronts. In Figure 2.10, then, the nature of demobilizing the opposition lobbying should aim to minimize the opposing leader's potential policy impact – that is, minimize the disparity between policies when he or she fights (say, f') and policies when he or she does not (say, f'') – and compensate the leader for the difference.

Developing this strategy further, it is worth reiterating that leading opponents' decision is not a calculus about fighting to get one's own preferences but rather fighting to get whatever the pivotal voter will ultimately support (f, or wherever f' would end up after being targeted by the White House's lobbying arsenal). Accordingly, the more pivotal voters' preferences match the president's proposal, the less incentive an opposing leader has to challenge that position (because he or she will get something close to it anyway). The first hypothesis for deterring the opposition, therefore, is somewhat surprising: the White House should *lobby pivotal voters to make them more supportive of the president's preferred position*. Notice that although behaviorally equivalent to a pure vote-centered lobbying strategy, here the White House's rationale for lobbying pivotal voters is not for their votes per se but rather to weaken leading opponents' bargaining posture.

Beyond pulling pivotal voters' preferences toward the president's position, an additional way in which the administration can lessen opposing leaders' incentive to fight the White House is to *convince leading opponents to dislike the president's position less* (to move O toward f). Importantly, this does not require that the White House induce leading opponents to support the president's position, much less vote for it. Instead, the administration need only convince opposing leaders that the effects of their counteroffensive would be minimal or, at least, could be better served elsewhere. Accordingly, the second deterring-the-opposition hypothesis is that the White House should *target leading opponents with the same lobbying tactics used in the legislative endgame*; the president should engage his leading opponents with arm-twisting and browbeating, private appeals and public pressure.

Of course, a third way to diminish leading opponents' incentive to fight is to *compromise the president's position* (offer f' instead of f''). This is not to say that the administration should capitulate all or even concede much; rather, the White House should compromise only enough to mollify leading opponents. Hence, this aspect of the demobilizing-leading-opponents hypothesis suggests that the White House should be willing to compromise with leading opponents, negotiating a "deal" that is more moderate than the best of the potentially passable policies but still better than what the president could get with an endgame floor fight. This is a point worth reiterating: the White House should only divert lobbying resources to leading opponents if doing so yields greater influence than would be possible through vote-centered lobbying alone.

This key point about agenda-centered lobbying leads to the final insight: because the president seeks a "deal" that is worse for leading opponents than what they could get by challenging him, the administration must *compensate these leading opponents* to offset the difference. This "horse-trading" can be on exogenous issues – for example, a different bill, an executive or judicial nomination, or some other executive-controlled offering – but often occurs within the confines of the same bill. Typically, the president's part of the logroll is included as the bill's first title, leading opponents' part as its second.

In sum, deterring leading opponents is an important if somewhat intricate page in a White House's legislative playbook. In seeking a favorable "deal" with leading opponents in the legislative earlygame (and avoiding a floor fight in the legislative endgame), an administration should use everything in its lobbying arsenal to undercut opponents' incentive to challenge the president and his proposal, or at least something close. White House staffers can do so, first, by lobbying swing voters to weaken opposing leaders' leverage; second, by persuading opposing leaders directly; and, finally, by offering them a combination of intrapolicy concessions and extrapolicy compensation. Notably, this agenda-centered lobbying strategy simultaneously affirms the pivotal voter's importance and offers a strategic path by which the president can circumvent it.

2.2.2.2 *The consequences of agenda-centered lobbying.* Unlike in vote-centered lobbying, where the White House's effectiveness depends just on the president's allocation of political capital and members' responsiveness to that expenditure, presidential influence from agenda-centered lobbying is more nuanced. In addition to the president's resource investment and members' reaction to it, presidents' potential impact from agenda-centered lobbying also depends on other players' preferences and the location of the status quo. Taken together, these factors mean that sometimes an agenda-centered strategy is not viable; other times it adds little to a vote-centered strategy; and occasionally it provides presidents with a much more effective path for promoting their agenda, allocating their resources, and exerting influence on Capitol Hill.

To start, it is worth recalling that the president's success turns on the preference distribution given rival alternatives. As such, an agenda-centered lobbying strategy becomes viable only as the status quo diverges from the pivotal voter's predisposition; otherwise, the status quo serves as a rival alternative that pivotal voters will prefer to virtually any presidential proposal – regardless of what opposing leaders propose (or don't). So if an agenda-centered lobbying strategy is to work, a necessary condition is that the status quo be not only far away from the president but also far from the pivotal voter. As such, through the rest of this section, I limit my analysis to the relevant class of cases – that is, cases where the status quo policy starts opposite the president's side and far from the pivotal voter's preferred position.

Figure 2.11 unpacks the president's potential policy influence from agenda-centered lobbying.[19] Here, the (conservative) president, P, seeks to replace a distant status quo, sq, with a new policy closer to his ideal. In doing so, he competes against a (liberal) opposition leader, O, for the pivotal voter's, f, support. As before, I turn the left–right ideological spectrum counterclockwise, producing a vertical axis of policy content that runs conservative to liberal, top to bottom. And again, the horizontal axis shows how much political capital the president invests in promoting this particular policy initiative. Finally, to help clarify the president's potential influence from executing an agenda-centered lobbying strategy, Figure 2.11 also displays

[19] Figure 2.11 reflects predictions derived from a fully formalized version of the theory (Beckmann and Kumar forthcoming). There, comparative statics analysis showed, "[often] a president can not only exert *greater influence* with an agenda-centered strategy than he could have with a vote-centered one, but doing so may actually require *less political capital* than a vote-centered strategy alone would have demanded" [emphasis in original] (21).

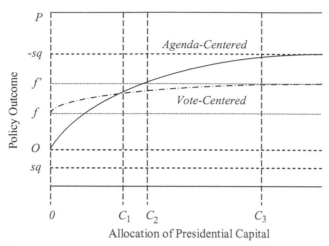

Figure 2.11 Presidential Influence via Agenda-Centered and Vote-Centered Lobbying.

the president's influence from vote-centered lobbying alone, detailed previously.

As has been the case throughout, when the president either lacks political capital or chooses not to use it, his only available option is getting some issue onto the congressional calendar. The president merely proposes his preferred policy, which leading allies and opponents then counter with proposals of their own. Although the president and each congressional leader wants to pass a bill as close to his or her ideal as possible, all end up settling on the pivotal voter's preference, f. So when unsupported by a White House lobbying offensive, the president's proposals will surrender to whatever outcome the House median and Senate filibuster pivot prefer.

In contrast, now let us look at cases where the president is motivated to lobby and has political capital to invest in the effort. Specifically, let me consider the president's policy impact across three levels of political capital: low, medium, and high. Because we have already seen that a nonlobbying president can pass the pivotal voter's preferred bill, I will use that baseline to assess what happens when the president does lobby – using a vote-centered strategy, an agenda-centered strategy, or both. Figure 2.11 does this by tracing what policy would pass if pivotal voters were lobbied with a vote-centered strategy, as well as what policy "deal" an opposing leader, O, would be willing to accept if targeted per an agenda-centered strategy.[20]

For cases where the president wants to lobby but has limited political capital to draw on ($0 < C < C_1$), looking back, Figure 2.11 affirms the intuitive: the president's legislative options are limited. Lacking enough capital to induce leaders to accept any sort of "deal" that is better than he could get from lobbying pivotal voters, the president and his staffers' only viable strategy is the vote-centered one. But, of course, even executing the vote-centered strategy does not yield much influence; the president simply does not have enough "juice" to substantially alter members' preferences or, in turn, the outcome.

The president's prospects improve substantially, though, when he allocates even modest levels of political capital ($C_1 < C < C_2$) to lobbying for a particular initiative. At this point – specifically, at C_1 – an agenda-centered strategy becomes viable. That is, with a medium investment of political capital, now the president has enough resources to get opposing leaders to cut a "deal" with the White House that is better than he could get from just lobbying pivotal voters. In fact, even with this rather modest infusion of political capital, C_1 to C_2, an agenda-centered lobbying strategy allows a president to exert even more influence than would be possible with a massive investment (up to C_3) in vote-centered lobbying. And granting the president even more political capital to invest in an issue ($C_2 < C$) only adds to an agenda-centered strategy's attractiveness and effectiveness compared to the more familiar vote-centered strategy.

Overall, the predicted impact of the president's agenda-centered lobbying is real, and potentially substantial, but also highly conditional. In contrast to a vote-centered strategy, which can be employed whenever a president is willing and able to invest lobbying resources in advocating an issue, the White House's agenda-centered strategy only applies with (1) a far-off status quo, and (2) a medium to large

---

[20] The analysis that follows assumes that all lawmakers, including opposing leaders and pivotal voters, respond equally to presidential lobbying. Obviously, when pivotal voters are more pliable than leading opponents, a vote-centered strategy becomes more effective, while agenda-centered lobbying becomes increasingly effective when leading opponents are more pliable than pivotal voters (see Beckmann and Kumar 2009).

supply of political capital. Absent these prerequisites, the president's fate turns on pivotal voters and his ability to influence them via vote-centered lobbying. But often these strategic stars do align – that is, the president is flush with political capital when seeking to change a distant status quo – and when they do, an agenda-centered strategy affords presidents not just a second path for exerting influence but also a better path. Indeed, under these favorable conditions, the president gets far more policy bang for his lobbying buck from an agenda-centered strategy than a vote-centered one – without having to prevail in an all-out floor fight for pivotal voters' support.

2.3   THE CONTOURS OF PRESIDENTIAL LEADERSHIP IN LAWMAKING

Unpacking the logic of presidents' strategies for exerting legislative influence has offered a new look at the presidential–congressional relationship, as well as novel predictions about its processes and its products. But if tracing presidents' lobbying options and potential influence has uncovered new insights from the president's point of view, stepping back helps reveal the bigger presidential–congressional picture. In this final theoretical section, then, I move away from the president's strategic perspective to examine all the conceptual pieces that go into the policymaking puzzle: some of which presidents can affect, many of which they cannot.

2.3.1   External Factors Affecting Presidential Success or Failure

The first of the factors that presidents cannot control but that still greatly affect their legislative prospects is also the most important: the status quo. As we have seen, a distant status quo is a necessary precursor to positive presidential power, and the more distant the status quo, the better the president's chances for replacing it with one he prefers. Of course, presidents cannot control their predecessors' policies. If a president happens to enter office after like-minded policymakers have already adjusted a myriad of distant status quos closer to pivotal voters' preferences, his prospects will flag. The same is true when the president himself succeeds in replacing old status quos with new policies early in his term. On the other hand, it only takes a few well-placed far-off status quos for a White House to see a lucrative set of legislative targets.

The second nonpresidential factor that shapes presidents' policy-making prospects is lawmakers' preferences, especially those of opposing leaders and pivotal voters. When it comes to the president's agenda, the more these strategically positioned lawmakers agree with him (or at least the less they differ), the better his chances for securing a favorable deal in the legislative earlygame and/or winning a key vote in the legislative endgame. By contrast, when leading opponents and swing voters resolutely oppose the president's plan, nothing the president or his aides can do will push his initiatives to passage. And, to be sure, presidents have very little say over Congress' composition, its leaders, or their predispositions.

Presidents' political capital comprises the final conceptual variable that is largely beyond their control. Pundits' analysis notwithstanding, ultimately presidents' standing is less affected by micro-level tactical maneuvers than by macro-level fundamentals: peace, prosperity, and public opinion. A popular president, bolstered by positive conditions, will find members more favorably disposed to his wishes; unpopular presidents serving during troubled times will not.

2.3.2 Internal Factors Affecting Presidential Success

Considering that the realm beyond presidents' rule is both vast and important, it is easy to see how much of a president's legislative record does not depend on him, his surrogates, or their actions. Yet I have argued that within their particular confines, presidents are far from helpless against the Congress and context they happen to confront. They have considerable control over the persuasive arrows in their office's tactical quiver, and each president's decisions about how best to utilize that lobbying arsenal can affect whether he wins or loses in Congress.

One important area where presidents have significant choice, unlike most lawmakers, is their policy agenda – that is, the issues that consume their attention. Whether presidents fill their agenda strategically can greatly affect their chances for signing their initiatives into law. Indeed, my theory suggests that among the issues presidents care about, the White House team does best when it targets its efforts in areas with distant status quos (and the more distant, the better). In doing so, presidents improve their policymaking possibilities, partly by expanding the range of policies on which pivotal voters might support the administration and partly by increasing the chances that opposing leaders might cut a "deal" favorable to the presidential preferences. Importantly, by smartly picking which status quos they will address, presidents can establish a firm bargaining position even when they face far-off pivotal voters, divided government, or both.

A second realm in which presidents have considerable discretion, and that implicates their success, is their lobbying operation. As the theory shows, presidential lobbying is not "one size fits all"; rather, each White House team must tailor its mix of lobbying strategies to fit its particular strategic situation. Because the optimal lobbying blend depends on a myriad of exogenous factors – including the location of the status quo, the nature of each side's leaders, pivotal voters' pre-dispositions, and the president's political capital – those White House teams deft at picking lobbying targets and executing lobbying tactics will best improve the president's legislative prospects, sometimes dramatically.

Regarding presidential coalition building, then, the picture that emerges is one where presidents' options are neither as boundless as pundits intimate nor as limited as political scientists have concluded. Instead, I predict that presidents confront a constrained-optimization problem. Factors beyond a president's control may be limiting, but they are not immutable, at least when the president invests his political capital in changing them. The trick for White House officials, then, is recognizing their situation and tailoring their lobbying resources to fit it.

However, although the White House's smart choice and effective execution of lobbying strategies always boost the president's chances for success, not all presidents will exert substantial influence. Even when expertly used, presidents' lobbying options do not always confer equivalent influence. Rather, each president's potential for plying lawmakers to secure success again depends on conditions beyond the White House's control. A president's impact is enhanced when he seeks to change far-off status quos, enjoys ample political capital, and confronts pliable leading opponents and/or pivotal voters. It is diminished when he strives to change centrist status quos, has little to no political capital, or confronts opposing leaders and pivotal voters who staunchly oppose his proposals.

2.4 EMPIRICAL IMPLICATIONS

Much of any theory's insight is revealed in its distinguishing predictions. As the final step in developing this book's overriding theory, it is therefore useful to spell out this new understanding's empirical implications for how we study presidential influence on Capitol Hill. Let me briefly highlight the most important points that have emerged.

John Kennedy once noted that presidential candidates tender positions on everything "from cranberries to creation" (17 January 1960). Certainly, the demand to articulate preferred positions only increases for the presidential candidate who actually wins. But not all revealed positions receive the same support from the White House. Most get nothing more than a mere comment; others are supported with the White House's "full-court press." In my theory, this selectivity matters. Indeed, the first empirical point of emphasis is that presidents' positive influence depends heavily on lobbying to work. Thus, my account affirms the advice of Richard Nixon's Attorney General, John Mitchell: "Watch what we do, not what we say."

The theory's second empirical implication for studying presidential influence highlights the president's ultimate objective: outcomes, not necessarily roll-call votes. Put differently, the White House wants to change the nation's laws, so the paramount metric of presidential success is the substantive result. And while political scientists lack any precise measure of policy content, the foremost empirical tests of presidents' influence should still highlight outcomes; they should address the ideological results of the legislative process.

But, of course, that presidents' influence is primarily manifest in substantive outcomes does not mean that its evidence cannot be seen in roll-call votes. Indeed, it should be; a requisite part of winning on the overall outcome is winning on the relevant votes. This is where my theory of presidential influence proves instructive. By showing that presidents' options for winning key votes often involve prevoting processes, it reveals that tests based exclusively on votes have missed

an important aspect of president-led coalition building. To account
for the remainder, researchers must account simultaneously for voting
and prevoting processes.

The final empirical point deserving mention has been reflected
throughout this chapter: studying presidents' positive role in lawmaking does not require accounting for each president's personal experience or idiosyncratic traits. The reason is that presidents' strategic
opportunities are constrained, their tactical resources limited (see
Edwards 1989; Jones 1994); therefore, as self-interested strategic
actors confronting a constrained-optimization problem, "most presidents [will] behave similarly in similar contexts" (Hager and Sullivan
1994, 1081). This is especially true as all modern presidents have filled
their lobbying shop with Washington's most experienced, successful operatives (Collier 1997). Accordingly, even "outsider" presidents
enjoy ample access to "insider" know-how and can act accordingly.

2.5 CONCLUSION

Modern presidents enter office having campaigned on an ambitious
legislative agenda, one they want to pass and are willing to promote
during their time in the White House. This chapter has proposed a
theory to explain the strategies by which presidents can best do just
that, as well as the factors that determine how well those strategies
work – or don't.

The theory's foremost contention is that presidents not only can
get their preferred initiatives considered but also can further encour-
age their passage via agenda-centered and vote-centered lobbying.
By tracking the logic motivating these strategies, as well as the consequences that follow, a more nuanced view of contemporary presidents'
role in U.S. lawmaking has emerged. Although presidents may sometimes engage in knock-down, drag-out floor fights for pivotal voters'
support, such endgame interactions are the exception rather than the
rule. More typical presidential–congressional relations, I have argued,
entail bargaining between the White House and congressional leaders
over what alternatives will make it to the floor. If a president can rally
leading allies' support and strike a "deal" with opposing leaders in the
legislative earlygame, he not only can circumvent a costly endgame

floor fight but also can actually sign into law a bill more to his liking than would have been possible by just waging an endgame offensive for aye votes.

The essence of presidential leadership, then, is the normal grist of legislative politics: arm-twisting, browbeating, and deal making. The challenge of presidential leadership is recognizing how best to target those efforts: toward beating leading opponents on floor votes or negotiating a deal with them before then. These decisions are not easy, and they require a nuanced understanding of how Washington works. But if a president and his team are able to tailor their lobbying to fit the issue, moment, and Congress they confront, presidents can help pick not only which problems lawmakers address but also which solutions they adopt.

Unpacking the logic and consequences of presidents' strategic choice of lobbying targets and tactics has shown us that presidential leadership in Congress looks quite different than it is popularly portrayed or has previously been tested. I now turn to examining these hypotheses. The following chapters test predictions about both the mechanisms of presidential influence (Chapter 3) and their manifestations – on key roll-call votes (Chapter 4) and on the content of new laws (Chapter 5).

CHAPTER THREE

Case Study: Pushing President Bush's 2001 Tax Cut

Even before entering the White House, George W. Bush and his top aides were plotting how to pass the incoming president's top legislative priority: revising the tax code to the tune of 1.6 trillion dollars. Fueling their efforts was President Bush's insistence that the goal was not passing *a* major tax cut but rather passing *his* major tax cut, as he noted at a Rose Garden launching event: "I urge the Congress to pass my tax relief plan with the swiftness these uncertain times demand. I will now sign a letter of transmittal, and soon hope I'll be signing the needed tax relief" (8 February 2001). The following day's *Washington Post* summarized the situation succinctly: "President Bush sent Congress a plan yesterday for the deepest federal income tax cut in 20 years and used a dire warning about the economy as opening ammunition in a legislative battle that could define his first year in office" (9 February 2001, A1).

Given the tax cut's high stakes and uncertain prospects, that President Bush emphasized devising and executing an effective "legislative strategy" seemed reasonable. After all, such strategic gaming has been a staple of White House decision making ever since Franklin Roosevelt advocated his New Deal agenda. Indeed, the basic question the Bush team considered early in 2001 is the same one all modern administrations have mulled over time and again: By what means can we best build winning congressional coalitions for the president's legislative proposals? Or, more operationally, *Whom should we lobby?* and *How should we lobby them?*

Drawing on the previous chapter's theoretical exposition, we now have predictions about how the Bush White House, like any other in the postwar period, should answer these core questions of presidential leadership. Tailoring their choice of targets and tactics to fit the policy issue the president cares about, the political context he inhabits, and the Congress he happens to confront, I predict that the administration should lobby a mix of pivotal voters (vote-centered lobbying) and congressional leaders (agenda-centered lobbying), focusing on the former when necessary and the latter when possible.

This chapter tests the predicted mechanisms of presidential influence by capitalizing on the research opportunity presented by the 2001 tax cut debate. After locating this case within the broader context of issues that presidents and lawmakers engage, I argue that the constellation of strategic factors before President's Bush's tax cut initiative afforded his administration substantial strategic discretion, substantial potential influence. Developing specific hypotheses about the White House's choice of lobbying targets and tactics in this case, I then turn to testing those predictions systematically. Results show that the White House's lobbying operation did follow the predicted strategies of presidential lobbying; the White House sought to mobilize leading allies, deter leading opponents, and attract swing voters.

3.1 THEORETICAL TENETS OF TAX CUTS IN THE 107TH CONGRESS

On the merits, President Bush's tax cut plan was an ambitious one. Beyond seeking to lower individual tax rates "across the board," Mr. Bush further hoped to enact several provisions long advocated by conservatives: tax cuts for dual-income married couples, reduced tax obligations on inheritances, added tax credits for children, permanent business tax offsets for research and development, and tax benefits for charitable contributions.[1] Taken as a whole, President Bush's tax package was nearly twice as large as a tax cut bill President Clinton

---

[1] The National Taxpayers Union (NTU) estimated that for the ten years implicated, President Bush's tax cut proposal would cut 6% of the total federal tax revenues, 1.1% of the nation's gross domestic product (GDP) (NTU Issue Brief 112, 2001, available at www.ntu.org). For perspective, 2001 federal spending on *all* discretionary domestic programs was 19.1% of the tax revenues and 3.1% of the GDP (Congressional Budget Office).

had previously vetoed because he viewed it as a "fiscally reckless tax strategy" (5 August 2000). What is more, updated estimates showed that President Bush's bill would cost the U.S. Treasury 25 percent more than thought during the 2000 campaign – when Albert Gore, the former Vice President and Democratic nominee for president, had pilloried the plan as a "risky tax scheme" that threatened the federal budget, especially the Social Security trust fund.[2]

Besides its vast policy implications, though, what made President Bush's tax cut proposal so striking was the political context in which it was offered. For one thing, Mr. Bush entered office having failed to win a majority of the popular vote (47.9 percent) and, in fact, without having even garnered a plurality (Mr. Gore received 48.4 percent). What's more, George Bush's victory in the Electoral College was far from clear-cut. Only when the U.S. Supreme Court, in a five-to-four decision, stopped an ongoing vote recount in Florida was Mr. Bush's 537-winning-vote margin affirmed, thereby guaranteeing him Florida's electoral votes, a majority in the Electoral College, and election as the Forty-Third President of the United States. So although elections occasionally confer a "mandate" that bolsters the president and his agenda, the 2000 presidential election was not one of them.

Adding to voters' tepid endorsement of a Bush presidency was their modest support for his proposed tax cut. Martin Wattenberg's (2004) research showed that although "the choice was crystal clear for all to see during the 2000 campaign – a big tax cut for everyone, or setting aside surplus funds for Social Security and Medicare in a lockbox... the degree to which this article finds that voters failed to understand the choices involved is stunning" (838–839). It was a

---

[2] Like the former president and vice president, analysts of all ideological stripes saw high stakes in the tax cut debate. Paul Krugman (2001), the progressive economist and *New York Times* columnist, penned an op-ed underscoring the point: "What do Medicare and the military have in common? Both are about to be betrayed in the name of tax cuts." Conservative Congressman Steven Largent (R-OK), despite having a different point of view, saw similar importance in the issue. He wrote, "In the week that Mr. Reagan turned 90, Mr. Bush served up a bold and truly Reaganesque proposal. . . . Simply put, this is a choice between squandering your surplus tax dollars on a bigger Washington at the expense of our economy, or putting some of that tax money back into the hands of taxpayers where it will help our economy. I choose the latter" (*The Washington Times*, 13 February 2001).

pattern that persisted after the election (Bartels 2005; Hacker and Pierson 2005; Jacobson 2004). When the Gallup Organization asked citizens whether they supported or opposed the president's tax cut plan, the portion answering "support" consistently ran around 55 percent. However, when further asked about diverting those same monies away from tax cuts and toward Social Security, Medicare, education, or other domestic programs, strong majorities supported doing so (2001 Gallup Poll). Notably, the public's appraisals did not change over time or in response to the Bush administration's aggressive "going-public" campaign (see Edwards 2003).

Then again, even if President Bush had enjoyed strong public support, he would still have been unlikely to find smooth sailing on Capitol Hill. Despite a Republican "majority" in each chamber, the margins were exceedingly close (50.9 percent in the House, 50.0 percent in the Senate), with the pivotal votes being held by ideological moderates.[3] The Senate's closer margins and looser rules made the president's prospects in the upper chamber especially daunting. The *Los Angeles Times* understated the president's comparative challenges in the Senate when explaining that "Senate rules make it harder to move legislation quickly" (31 January 2001).

In short, the policy stakes and political circumstances surrounding the 2001 tax cuts offer an especially clean look at a White House's legislative strategy. Anticipating that an intense legislative battle was in the offing – one the administration entered without a clear electoral mandate or intense popular support – the White House invested heavily to develop and implement an effective lobbying strategy. The Bush team's choices of lobbying targets and tactics in support of the president's tax cut bill, therefore, reflect the careful judgment of seasoned White House operatives on an important, controversial domestic policy initiative. Because these are exactly the judgments theorized about in Chapter 2, let me now map this case's empirical referents to the theory's conceptual components to derive specific predictions about the White House lobbying choices in this case.

---

[3] The Senate was actually divided fifty–fifty, Republican–Democratic. However, because Vice President Cheney provided the president's fellow partisans with the tie-breaking vote, the Republicans initially held "majority" party status.

3.1.1 The Status Quo

If there is one factor that most determines a president's prospects for success, it is the location of the status quo. Unfortunately, political scientists have yet to devise a method for accurately knowing where any given status quo is located.[4] Instead, the best approximations have looked at *ex post* voting coalitions to infer *ex ante* status quo locations (assuming that those closest to it opposed proposed changes). However, this approach indicates only from which ideological side the status quo started, not its exact position.

Despite the lack of a metric that precisely locates a status quo's ideological position, there is good reason to believe that in the case of the 2001 tax cuts, the status quo was extremely liberal, or at least equivalent to being extremely liberal. Two points, in particular, made this so. The first was federal budget estimates, updated just after President Bush took office, showing that the government would take in substantially more revenues than needed to pay its yearly obligations. The effect was to render "doing nothing" (i.e., keeping the status quo) equivalent to growing the size of government – dramatically. Richard Stevenson's (2001) contemporaneous analysis in *The New York Times* underscores the point: "The Congressional Budget Office's new, upwardly revised surplus projection to $5.6 trillion over the next decade makes it particularly hard for Democrats to sustain their argument that there is not room for a broad-based tax cut."

The second reason the status quo tax policy seemed extremely liberal in early 2001 stemmed from early symptoms of an economic slowdown. Although President Clinton's *Economic Report of the President for 2001*, issued only days before he left office, argued that the economy's fundamentals were strong, *The New York Times* noted, "Many economists on Wall Street have been marking down their forecasts in recent weeks and concluding that the risks of a recession are growing" (12 January 2001). A February 12, 2001, *Washington Post* headline reflected the growing sentiment: "Economy's Vital Signs Weaken; Price, Confidence News Send Stocks Plunging." For lawmakers, the symptoms of a flagging economy served to highlight that keeping surplus monies in the public till was an unsavory option. Indeed, there

---

4 See Smith (2007, chap. 6) for a thoughtful discussion of this point.

is good reason to believe that centrist lawmakers found the status quo tax code less preferable than any number of alternatives, including a major tax cut.

3.1.2 Supportive Leaders' Preferences

Throughout this theoretical section, I have argued that presidents and their leading allies should usually work hand-in-glove to promote their shared preferences. The exceptions to this general rule arrive only under a somewhat uncommon confluence: the status quo is extreme *and* the president's leading allies might propose a policy more moderate than his. However, looking at the 2001 tax cuts suggests that this was one of those cases, at least potentially. Having already shown the status quo to be extreme, let me briefly explain why the White House could not take for granted its leading allies' unwavering concurrence with President Bush's preferences (see Table 3.1).

In the House of Representatives, although Speaker Dennis Hastert (R-IL) and Majority Leader Dick Armey (R-TX) quickly expressed their support of the president's proposal and affirmed their intention to help promote it, Ways and Means Chairman Bill Thomas (R-CA) sounded a more cautious tone, at least initially. Only weeks before President Bush's inauguration, Chairman Thomas said in an interview, "The tax question obviously is a difficult one. Given the results of the election, no one is going to get everything they want. Our goal is to sit down and put a package together that has a chance of becoming law" (*The NewsHour with Jim Lehrer*, 5 January 2001). *The New York Times* picked up the Chairman's lukewarm signal: "Mr. Thomas's failure to offer full-throated support for Mr. Bush's proposal was the latest sign that Congressional Republicans were troubled by the plan" (6 January 2001).

To be sure, the uncertainty the White House had about their House leaders' commitment to the president's plan paled in comparison to the anxiety spawned by their Senate leaders. Both conservative, Majority Leader Trent Lott (R-MS) and Finance Chairman Charles Grassley (R-IA) were also widely regarded as so-called deal cutters – that is, members who readily sacrifice ideological purity for smooth passage. So when Chairman Grassley said of the president's proposal,

TABLE 3.1. *Leading allies' ideological and electoral traits, 107th Congress*

	107th Congress ideological score[a] (liberal to conservative, -1 to $+1$)	2000 Bush electoral margin[b] (% Bush – % Gore)
House[c]		
Speaker Dennis Hastert (R-IL)	0.49	+17
Majority Leader Dick Armey (R-TX)	0.57	+44
Ways & Means Chairman Bill Thomas (R-CA)	0.39	+31
Senate[c]		
Majority Leader Trent Lott (R-MS)	0.49	+ 15
Majority Whip Don Nickles (R-OK)	0.66	+22
Finance Chairman Charles Grassley (R-IA)	0.37	−1

[a] Ideological scores come from Keith Poole and Howard Rosenthal's estimates based on members' roll-call votes vis-à-vis their colleagues. Details of these analyses are available at their Web site (www.voteview.com).

[b] The electoral margin included is that among the member's constituents: the district for representatives, the state for senators.

[c] Based on preliminary interviews with former White House staffers, leadership members were deemed to be each chamber's top two floor leaders and relevant committee leader. The relevant committees are the House Ways and Means and the Senate Finance committees.

"I don't think it would fly right today," the president's aides had good reason to worry that Mr. Grassley (and, in turn, Mr. Lott) would start looking for one that could (*The New York Times*, 6 January 2001).

In summary, as 2001 commenced, President Bush's leading legislative allies sent signals that they were open to bills more moderate than the one the president would offer. Given that the extreme status quo meant the president had the potential to do better, my theory suggests that such early signs of moderation should have thrown up red flags inside the West Wing. At the same time, the president's leading allies were ideologically conservative, and all but Senator

Grassley came from constituencies that strongly supported President Bush. So while getting their own congressional leaders "onboard" with President Bush's tax preferences should have been priority one, on balance the White House had reason to expect that such efforts would ensure that they eventually were.

3.1.3 Opposing Leaders' Preferences

Offsetting any anxiety President Bush had about his supportive leaders' fidelity to his position, opposing leaders' relatively moderate posture should have generated substantial hopefulness throughout the administration. Indeed, I have argued that the White House's best opportunity for exerting influence in Congress comes when they confront "pliable" opposing leaders – and, at least in the Senate (which, as noted, promised to be the more challenging chamber), there was good reason to believe this is what the White House had.

Table 3.2 lists Democratic leaders' personal ideological scores along with President Bush's electoral margin among their constituents. The former reveal each member's ideological predisposition relative to the conservative president; the latter highlights their basic standing electoral incentive vis-à-vis President Bush. What jumps out is that Democratic leaders in the House were generally liberal and from an anti-Bush constituency anyway. Indeed, all three were more liberal than the median Democratic representative, and only Representative David Bonier (D-MI) came from a district that President Bush had carried in the recently concluded election. A group likely to cut a deal favorable to President Bush it was not.

Contrasted with their House counterparts, the Senate's Democratic leaders were ideologically centrist and politically conflicted. All three Democratic leaders were more moderate than the median Democratic senator, and each came from a state that President Bush had won only months before. In fact, the Democrats' foremost floor and committee leaders came from states that President Bush had carried by huge margins, fifteen and twenty-four points, respectively. If a White House does, in fact, consider leading opponents as potential lobbying targets, the Senate's Democratic leaders would appear to be attractive ones. To be sure, their ideological predispositions and electoral incentives

TABLE 3.2. *Leading opponents' ideological and electoral traits, 107th Congress*

	107th Congress ideological score[a] (liberal to conservative, −1 to +1)	2000 Bush electoral margin[b] (% Bush − % Gore)
House[c]		
Minority Leader Dick Gephardt (D-MO)	−0.51	−5
Minority Whip David Bonier (D-MI)	−0.55	+1
Ways & Means ranking member Charles Rangel (D-NY)	−0.52	−84
Senate[c]		
Minority Leader Thomas Daschle (D-SD)	−0.39	+15
Minority Whip Harry Reid (D-NV)	−0.37	+3
Finance ranking member Max Baucus (D-MT)	−0.21	+24

[a] Ideological scores come from Keith Poole and Howard Rosenthal's estimates based on members' roll-call votes vis-à-vis their colleagues. Details of these analyses are available at their Web site (www.voteview.com).

[b] The electoral margin included is that among the member's constituents: the district for representatives, the state for senators.

[c] Based on preliminary interviews with former White House staffers, leadership members were deemed to be each chamber's top two floor leaders and relevant committee leader. The relevant committees are the House Ways and Means and the Senate Finance committees.

offered reason to believe that they might prefer earlygame deal cutting to endgame floor fighting.

3.1.4 Pivotal Voters' Preferences

The final theoretically key group of lawmakers is the one most often highlighted by political scientists: pivotal voters. Again, these are the handful of members whose preferences relative to their colleagues make them especially likely to decide which rival alternative passes. And precisely because these swing members get to decide whose bill will prevail, pivotal voters' influence spans across the process, from earlygame strategizing to endgame decision making. Because President Bush, his advisors, and his leading allies decided to push his tax

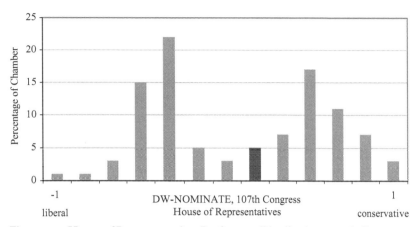

Figure 3.1 House of Representatives Preference Distribution, 107th Congress.
Source: Keith Poole and Howard Rosenthal (www.voteview.com).
*Darkest bar indicates location of House's median member, the "pivotal" voter in the 2001 tax cut debate.

cut proposal through the budget reconciliation process, which does not allow filibusters, the pivotal voter in each chamber was its median.[5]

Looking at members' ideological preferences in the 107th Congress, running from liberal (−1) to conservative (+1), we see that both the House (Fig. 3.1) and the Senate (Fig. 3.2) exhibited the polarized patterns that have characterized the capitol in recent years. In each body, there was a large cluster of conservatives and a large cluster of liberals, with a small cadre of "moderates" in between. The 107th Congress largely reflected Jim Hightower's (1997) colorful adage, "There's nothing in the middle of the road but yellow stripes and dead armadillos."

Although Congress may have had so-called centrists in short supply, the relative ideological balance around them left each chamber's few moderates in a decisive position. On the tax cuts, at least, it was the lonely members in the middle who held the "pivotal" votes. As indicated by the darker bar in Figures 3.1 and 3.2, each chamber's median member was near the ideological center, with the House's

---

[5] The budget reconciliation process allows lawmakers to budget for different policy areas (and certain bills) before actually authorizing money. Bills debated through this process cannot be filibustered, meaning that the simple majority rule governs their fate in both the House and the Senate.

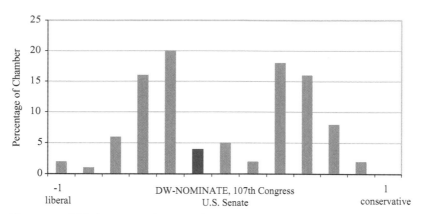

Figure 3.2 U.S. Senate Preference Distribution, 107th Congress.
Source: Keith Poole and Howard Rosenthal (www.voteview.com).
*Darkest bar indicates location of the median senator, the "pivotal" voter in the 2001 tax cut debate.

median member just right of center and the Senate's swing senator just left of center.

Taking a closer look at the lawmakers most likely to cast the "pivotal" vote on President Bush's tax cut plan, Table 3.3 lists the House and Senate members nearest the median. As the table makes clear, in addition to being ideologically moderate, these centrist legislators tended to confront countervailing partisan and electoral pressures. Among the House members, Republicans Nancy Johnson (R-CT), Chris Shays (R-CT), and Chris Smith (R-NJ) all came from districts that voted against President Bush, as did the Democrat, Jim Traficant (D-OH). Perhaps the most valuable target from the White House's perspective, therefore, was Amo Houghton (R-NY), whose moderate ideology was accented by a shared party affiliation and a constituency that supported the president.

The median senators exhibited similar countervailing interests, although with some interesting differences compared to their House colleagues. Contrary to the House's median voters, the Senate's swing senators were (somewhat) more liberal and included more Democrats. However, those Democrats – John Breaux (D-LA), Ben Nelson (D-NE), and Zell Miller (D-GA) – came from states that strongly supported President Bush in the 2000 election. The Republican swing senators, by contrast, represented constituents who preferred Al Gore to

TABLE 3.3. *Median voters' ideological and electoral traits, 107th Congress*

	107th Congress ideological score[a] (liberal to conservative, -1 to $+1$)	2000 Bush electoral margin[b] (% Bush – % Gore)
House		
Nancy Johnson (R-CT)	0.18	−10
Amo Houghton (R-NY)	0.18	+10
Chris Shays (R-CT)	0.19	−14
James Traficant (D-OH)	0.19	−20
Chris Smith (R-NJ)	0.20	−7
Senate		
John Breaux (D-LA)	−0.11	+8
Lincoln Chaffee (R-RI)	−0.09	−29
Ben Nelson (D-NE)	−0.06	+30
Jim Jeffords (R-VT)[c]	−0.01	−10
Zell Miller (D-GA)	0.03	+12

Note: Considered under budget reconciliation rules, both chambers decided the tax cut debate by simple majority rule, meaning that each body's pivotal voter was its median. To capture the legislators most likely to cast the pivotal vote, therefore, I show the five members nearest the median using their ideological scores.

[a] Ideological scores come from Keith Poole and Howard Rosenthal's estimates based on members' roll-call votes vis-à-vis their colleagues. Details of these analyses are available at their Web site (www.voteview.com).

[b] The electoral margin included is that among the member's constituents: the district for representatives, the state for senators.

[c] Catching the capitol by surprise, on May 24, 2001, Senator Jim Jeffords declared his intention to switch his party affiliation from Republican to Independent. Because this change took effect after the tax cut debate, however, Senator Jeffords' preswitch ideological score is used here.

George Bush. So despite their moderate ideology, the support of neither Democratic nor Republican swing senators was a given; they were "up for grabs."

All told, then, we can now see clearly why the 2001 tax cuts offer an especially good case for examining the full range of presidents' lobbying. On an important question of public policy, President Bush proposed a clear, if controversial, answer. As President Bush lacked the electoral clout, popular support, or partisan coalition to help make his case with lawmakers, his senior advisors believed that lobbying efforts would prove decisive, especially in the Senate. Indeed, they put a premium on developing an effective strategy to target the presidency's persuasive arsenal. Returning to the theory of president-led coalition building, we can now understand the logic motivating their effort.

3.2   PRESIDENT BUSH'S TAX CUT STRATEGY

Surveying the broader strategic landscape, President Bush and his congressional liaison staff could see that, despite the capitol's extreme polarization, both chambers' decisive votes were likely to be cast by a bipartisan group of cross-pressured moderates. The White House's challenge, therefore, was divining a strategy to win those swing legislators' support.

Given the constellation of key factors (delineated in the preceding section), I predict that the 2001 tax cut debate was one particularly favorable for presidential leadership. The combination of a far-off status quo and relatively supportive leading allies offered the possibility that the president could score a big win, a potential bolstered because each chamber's pivotal voters seemed "pliable." Add to these elements that the Senate's opposing leaders were ideologically moderate and electorally conflicted, and this was about as good a legislative opportunity as President Bush could have hoped for given the close margins. If the debate ended with a knock-down, drag-out floor fight, those in the West Wing had good reason to think they could win it. Greater still was the chance that President Bush could do even better: avoid a floor flight by cutting a deal with opposing leaders in the Senate. Let me explain.

3.2.1   Vote-Centered Lobbying (the Endgame Strategy)
Although pivotal members' moderate predispositions were not especially encouraging for President Bush's staffers, given that most of these lawmakers either were fellow partisans or had constituents who supported the president, or both, left the potential that they might be receptive to presidential persuasion. As such, the White House's first coalition-building strategy was not an altogether unsavory one: the president's team could seek to build a winning vote coalition by lobbying pivotal voters. Such an endgame strategy would start with each chamber's median member and, as he or she moved toward the president, include the interval between the median member and some

point closer to the president. Following the tenets of a vote-centered strategy, therefore, the representatives and senators identified previously should be singularly lucrative lobbying targets. Indeed, as part of an endgame offensive, the White House should hit these swing voters with the full array of persuasive tactics, from personal arm-twisting to public browbeating, as well as offering them various extrapolicy goodies and intrapolicy concessions.

3.2.2   Agenda-Centered Lobbying (The Earlygame Strategy)

But if the endgame strategy comprised one potential path for pushing President Bush's tax bill, it was not the only one, or even the best one. Instead of targeting pivotal voters one by one, the other way the administration could build a winning legislative coalition was to target congressional leaders – rallying leading allies' support and undercutting leading opponents' challenges. If successful, the White House could broker a three-party "deal" among the White House and leaders that left pivotal voters choosing between two suboptimal alternatives: the bipartisan "deal" or "nothing at all."

3.2.2.1 Mobilizing leading allies. Of course, before looking to cut a deal with leading opponents, President Bush and his team first had to make sure their leading allies' preferences would not undercut the president's. As noted previously, this was not an especially pressing worry, even though President Bush's congressional leaders – in both Houses, but especially the Senate – sent early signals that they might be willing to compromise. At the end of the day, the president's leading allies were personally predisposed to support the conservative policy and politically predisposed to support President Bush. As such, the White House should have targeted their leading allies using various persuasive tactics in order to get (and keep) them trained on the president's preference. This intraparty bargaining should span the entire process, as the crux of the administration's efforts here is not winning these supporters' votes but rather ensuring that they do not make policy concessions beyond what the president approves.

In addition to shoring up their supportive leaders' fidelity to the president's proposal, the White House and its legislative allies should also share policy information and political intelligence: even when the administration and its congressional leaders agree on their policy wishes, they still need to coordinate about how best to promote that policy. Importantly, such coordination should occur only with supportive leaders. With all other lawmakers, the administration bargains to change their positions and does not coordinate to promote it.

3.2.2.2 *Deterring leading opponents.* As consolidating and coordinating leading allies' support is the first prong of an agenda-centered lobbying strategy, the second prong entails deterring leading opponents' challenges. As noted, the House Democratic leaders were unlikely to be deterred, even if put squarely in the White House's lobbying crosshairs. As they were liberal to start with and lacked any compelling reasons to change (e.g., a pro-Bush constituency), the odds were long that these opposing House leaders would make a tax cut deal that favored the president's position. In the lower chamber, therefore, much contact between the Bush administration and their leading opponents would not have been expected.

The situation in the Senate was different. There, the president had cause to think that the administration's lobbying could induce leading opponents to accept losses in tax cut policy in return for gains elsewhere. The challenge for the president's team, therefore, was to minimize these opposing senatorial leaders' perceptions of the costs to be incurred and maximize their perceptions of the benefits to be gained by striking a deal. Let me elaborate.

To decrease Senate Democratic leaders' incentive to fight, President Bush's lobbyists should first seek to undercut their bargaining leverage. The most obvious way to do this, I argued before, was to convince these leaders that there was little to be gained by eschewing earlygame negotiations for an endgame floor fight. Thus, I expect the White House should have lobbied the Senate's swing voters, not for their votes per se but rather as part of a campaign to weaken Senate Democratic leaders' bargaining position. In this way, the White House's lobbying logic is somewhat intricate. The administration's aim to change pivotal voters' preferences is not to prepare for the floor (although it is essentially a down payment toward that end) but rather to facilitate a deal with opposing leaders before then.

Beyond indirectly deterring the Senate's opposition leaders by lobbying the upper chamber's pivotal voters, the White House should also have aimed lobbying arrows at them directly. Indeed, from personal pitches to public pressure, the administration's bargaining resources should have been deployed to persuade leading opponents. If successful, this lobbying onslaught not only could have helped bring leading opponents to the bargaining table but also could have decreased their demands once there.

After pushing them as close to the president's side as possible, administration officials should then have turned to the final piece of the earlygame strategy: they should have negotiated a "deal" with these opposing leaders that gave President Bush more than pivotal voters would have allowed, much less preferred. This would have meant adding elements that leading opponents valued, making concessions on provisions they strongly opposed, and working out "agreements" on extrapolicy matters, such as other policy areas, presidential appointments, and even campaign activities (for or against).

3.3 TESTING THE WHITE HOUSE'S LOBBYING OPERATION

Its somewhat elaborate logic notwithstanding, applying the theory of presidential coalition building to the 2001 tax cut debate reveals straightforward empirical predictions about whom the White House should have lobbied and to what end. In both chambers, I expect the administration would have targeted (1) leading allies to best position the president's proposal, and (2) pivotal voters to help increase their support for it. In the Senate, I also predict that the White House should have lobbied (3) leading opponents to deter their challenges.

As plain as these hypotheses may be, the opposite is true about testing them. Even with daily coverage in major newspapers, there are no systematic records chronicling conversations between White House officials and various legislators' offices. If anything, the meetings that make their way into the news tend to reflect the most unusual, most dramatic interactions, not the typical ones that constitute the bedrock of the presidential–congressional relationship (see Andres, Griffin, and Thurber 2000; Beckmann 2008; Thurber 2006). What's more, the private documents of White House staffers are highly selective, if records are kept at all. The result is that researchers cannot merely rely on public reports or private records and presume that they accurately reflect the overall interaction patterns between executive and legislative officials.

Unfortunately, filling this empirical void is no small chore. For one thing, most so-called presidential–congressional interactions actually occur at staff levels – levels that include hundreds of relevant aides. Moreover, the vast majority of conversations occur in private, behind closed doors or over the phone. So not only are there no comprehensive records of presidential–congressional interactions, but gathering such data requires one account for both public and private interactions among both public officials and their respective staffs. As I say, an easy assignment it is not.

Recognizing these empirical obstacles, in this part of the study my overriding objective was to collect valid data on the quantity and quality of presidential lobbying. In the face of a nonexistent (or, at least, unreliable) archival record, the only prospect for gathering such data is to interview those individuals who know about presidential–congressional interactions, including those occurring at staff levels and in private. In practice, this meant I had to sit down with the staffers who served as relevant officers' "point people" on tax issues. As it is these individuals' job to synthesize everyone's goings-on on a daily basis, they know who is interacting with whom and they know what these interactions entail.

As accessing the information (via well-positioned individuals) is the first step in collecting valid data, the second step is to devise a way to accurately operationalize that information. To this end, specificity is key. That is, the best way to get valid data is to develop and implement measures in a context that maps onto the real world in which the lobbying interactions occur.[6] Because this research design trades breadth

---

[6] The strategy of maximizing validity by anchoring empirics to a particular case is commonplace. The National Election Studies, for example, ask respondents about their preferences on particular issues, candidates, parties, and such in a particular election (rather than issues, candidates, and parties in the abstract). Thus, they asked respondents about their preference between Reagan and Mondale in 1984, not about incumbents and challengers or Republicans and Democrats generally. Although this limits the data's scope in some ways, the gain in validity more than makes up for any loss in generality.

for depth, I tried to mitigate this drawback by focusing my tests on the most novel and controversial predictions – that the White House can often exert greater influence by targeting leaders (to manipulate policy alternatives) than by lobbying pivotal voters (to change preferences). Operationally, this meant anchoring the empirics to a major, controversial domestic issue – in this case, the 2001 tax cuts – and focusing on the White House's lobbying in the Senate, which is where I expected the administration to emphasize an earlygame strategy.[7] It is also where White House officials anticipated a tougher time passing the president's plan.

3.3.1   The Senate

In important ways, the U.S. Senate presents a hard test for my principal hypotheses. The first and most obvious is that the upper chamber is where my most novel predictions will play out, meaning that it is also where contrary results are most likely. Beyond that basic point, though, is that the Senate – famously revered as a deliberative body – affords its members a myriad of institutionally codified prerogatives to wield in legislative battles. Because my argument builds from the assumption that congressional leaders' agenda-setting capacity is an important stylistic feature of the policymaking process, here again the Senate provides a more difficult testing ground for my theory.

One potential concern about studying the Senate in 2001 is that it was "like no other time," according to Senator Tom Daschle's (D-SD) memoir. While any particular Congress has its idiosyncratic features and events, the 107th congressional term does stand out as being extraordinary.[8] However, these atypical events occurred after the tax

---

7   It is noteworthy, however, that while my research strategy emphasizes the importance of validity and specificity, this does not mean the research design is idiosyncratic to a particular case. Indeed, with only minor modifications, the general design and specific measures used here could easily be adapted to fit other cases – e.g., a different issue or chamber.

8   Illustrative of this point, on May 23, 2001, Senator Jim Jeffords (VT) announced that he would switch his partisan affiliation from Republican to Independent, thereby giving Democrats "majority" party status. And, even more important, on the morning of September 11, 2001, Al-Qaeda terrorists, in the worst act of domestic terrorism in U.S. history, hijacked and crashed commercial planes into the World Trade Center Towers, the Pentagon, and a field in Shanksville, Pennsylvania.

cut bill was debated, passed, and signed. Thus, the portion of the
107th Senate studied here is typical of Washington politics over the
last several decades, at least in matters of domestic policy.

3.3.2 The Sample

As noted previously, the best way to access information about
presidential–congressional interactions is to cull from people with
direct knowledge of them. Because it would be too cumbersome for
White House officials to divulge the number and nature of their meetings with each senator and his or her staff, I instead decided to gather
the lobbying information from the congressional side – that is, from
specific senators' "point people" in the 2001 tax cut debate. In deciding exactly which senators' offices to include in the study, I developed
a sampling frame to capture theoretically important variations, which
included the following:

- six of seven senators closest to the filibuster pivot
- six of seven senators closest to the median voter[9]
- twelve of sixteen nonleader Finance Committee members
- six of six committee and party leaders
- fifteen other Democrats
- fifteen other Republicans

In seeking interviews with the sampled senators (via their staffs),
I experienced just three refusals, all from Democratic backbenchers.
I replaced those senators by resampling within that stratum.[10] Additionally, I was unable to contact one aide who had left Washington for
a different job. The result was a response rate better than 90 percent,
which did yield a representative sample.

This correspondence between the population and my sample is
shown in Figure 3.3, which displays the distributions of both groups'

---

[9] The sample ended up including the five senators nearest the median. Per the advice
of colleagues, these five members are the "pivotal voters" in the following analyses.

[10] In supplementary interviews with White House staffers (see the following), I asked
whether the administration had "dealt much with [the senators who refused inter-
views]." Their answers indicated nothing unusual; differences between senators who
refused and those who took their places were negligible.

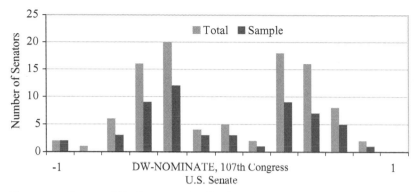

Figure 3.3 Senators' Preference Distribution, in Sample and Total.

ideological predispositions (see Poole and Rosenthal 1997). Plain to see, the patterns are quite similar.[11]

To augment the Capitol Hill interviews, I also conducted more than a dozen interviews with current and former White House officials. Five of these were people who served as senior-level aides (i.e., assistant to the president), and several others included their deputies. These interviews included officials from the Office of Legislative Affairs, the National Economic Council, and the Office of Management and Budget, as well as one high-ranking official from the Treasury Department.[12]

3.3.3 The Measures

Having explained the basic tenets of my research strategy – that is, to interview a stratified random sample of Senate staffers regarding the quantity and quality of their office's interactions with the White House during the 2001 tax cut debate – I can finally turn to delineating the actual measures used with those people about those

[11] To check whether my sample was representative of the full chamber for tax issues in particular, I conducted a similar comparison using National Taxpayer Union's Senate "ratings" for the 107th Congress. Results again showed the sample closely reflected the population. In fact, the mean NTU score overall is 46.6 (standard deviation [SD], 34.5); the mean score for senators in my sample is 44.9 (SD, 34.2). The difference is not statistically significant.

[12] Although the Office of Management and Budget and the National Economic Council are technically in the Executive Office of the President, functionally they worked as White House agents in this case. For simplicity, I refer to all the administration officials who lobbied on the president's behalf as White House staffers.

interactions. To that end, a few preliminary conceptual points are instructive.

The first is that presidential lobbying, like political participation and analogous concepts in political science, is not limited to one activity. Instead, it includes a variety of activities that, taken together, comprise the White House's repertoire for promoting the president's policy preferences. Or, put differently, presidential lobbying is a class of tactics. In this way, I make an analytic distinction between lobbying strategies and lobbying tactics. Lobbying *strategies* are the general prescriptions for how a White House can best use its resources to pass the president's preferred policy without regard to a particular legislative context; lobbying *tactics*, by contrast, are the specific techniques, practices, and methods employed to carry out a lobbying strategy in a particular instance. In other words, lobbying tactics are the behavioral manifestations of more general, latent lobbying strategies.

The second important point is that presidential lobbying encompasses more than just the president's personal lobbying activities; it also includes the activities of all those who "serve at the pleasure of the president." In this way, the concept might be better labeled presidency lobbying. But because institutions do not lobby – people do – I chose the more personal term of presidential lobbying. The point remains, though, that the concept of presidential lobbying involves not only the president per se but also all those whose position and performance are directly attributable to their service on his behalf.

3.3.3.1 Measuring White House lobbying: quantity. To measure the quantity of lobbying contacts, I asked the relevant Senate staffers the following question: "For any given issue, the White House can call on a whole host of people to work with Senators and their staffs regarding legislation. This can range from the president himself to his advisors, from Cabinet members to agency staff. So I guess my first question is, Who were you talking to in the administration?"

While introducing this question, I handed respondents a form that listed the administration officials who were active on the tax cut bill.[13] This form asked the aide to "Please check off the category that best reflects the number of conversations – face-to-face or on the phone – that your Senator and his/her staff had with the following people regarding the 2001 tax cut." The categories provided were none (0), a couple of times (1–3), several times (4–8), many times (9–15), and repeatedly (>15).[14] When respondents checked that they had more than 15 contacts with a particular White House official (or his or her staff), I further asked them to estimate how many conversations people in their office actually had with that official and/or his or her staff. The way we did this was to estimate, "On average, how many conversations took place in the weeks leading up to the markup? In the weeks leading up to the floor debate? In the weeks after the floor debate?" Combining those answers with the length of time captured by each period, I inferred the total number of conversations between a particular White House official and each senator and his or her staff. The result is that my dependent variable is an interval-level estimate of the number of contacts between various White House officials and each senator.

3.3.3.2 Measuring White House lobbying: quality. After getting answers regarding their number of contacts, I transitioned the interview to the nature of those contacts. I would say:

Now that I have a sense of the extent of your interactions with the administration, what I'd now like to turn to is talking a bit

---

[13] My list of "White House advocates" was determined in preliminary interviews with two White House staffers – one from the National Economic Council and the other from the Office of Management and Budget. I presented each with a list of all the offices inside the Executive Office of the President, as well as each Cabinet department, asking him or her to "put a check next to those offices that had any contacts with anyone in the Senate – including staffers." Both did so. Their responses were exactly the same except for two departments – Department of Agriculture and Department of Health and Human Services – which only one person thought had contacts. Any office receiving even one check was included on the form I presented to the Senate staffers.

[14] A comparable measure was initially developed and tested by Richard Hall for interactions between lobbyists and legislators (see Hall and Beckmann 2004; Hall and Miler 2008). I modified it here to account for the administration's various components and greater lobbying capacity.

more about the nature of those interactions. You know, political scientists frequently refer to "presidential–congressional relations," yet we actually know very little about what that means. So what I want to try to do here is more precisely specify the nature of your interactions with the White House.

During this preface, I handed the respondent a new form that listed a myriad of activities corresponding to my two basic tactic classes: bargaining and coordination. For each activity, I asked the staffer to "please rate the effort White House advocates exerted in their dealings with your Senator or his/her staff." The categories offered were none at all (0), a little (1), and a lot (2).

Turning to the specific items measured, as noted, they can be categorized into two basic classes: bargaining and coordination. The bargaining tactics include activities aimed at pressuring members (directly via persuasion or indirectly via going public) and/or compensating them (within the policy via modifying or outside the policy via exchanging). The coordination tactics, employed not to change a member's policy preference but rather to coordinate how best to promote it, include activities like sharing policy information and political intelligence. All these tactics are listed in Table 3.4. My two measures regarding lobbying quality thus reveal the average amount of bargaining and coordination between the administration and each senator's office. The potential answers range from 0 (no effort using any of the respective tactics) to 2 (a major effort using all of the respective tactics).

One final point worth noting here is that I showed the list of these lobbying activities to six current and former White House officials (most of whom served in the White House's Office of Legislative Affairs). I asked them: "In looking over these activities, how well does it seem to classify the types of things that go on between White House officials and people on Capitol Hill?" The universal answer was that if it was not exhaustive, it was close. One senior official declared, "Gee, this is really interesting. I'm trying to think of one example of a conversation that wouldn't fit in here . . . so far I haven't come up with anything." Another (deputy-level aide) offered, "This is really good. I think you've pretty much got it all on here – certainly all the big things."

TABLE 3.4. *Tactics included to measure the nature of the White House's lobbying*

Bargaining tactics[a]

"When dealing with your Senator and/or staff, did the White House . . .
  ". . . argue the policy merits?"
  ". . . argue the importance to the President and/or party?"
  ". . . argue the popularity of the President and/or his policy?"
  ". . . propose to offer (or threaten to withhold) the President's help
    on a different bill or on a peripheral provision?"
  ". . . propose to offer (or threaten to withhold) the President's help in an
    electoral campaign or with fundraising?"
  ". . . propose to offer (or threaten to withhold) a personal favor?"
  ". . . mobilize a grassroots campaign in your state?"
  ". . . mobilize important interest groups to contact your Senator in support
    of the President?"
  ". . . generate news coverage in your state?"
  ". . . mobilize state party leaders or public officials to contact your Senator
    in support of the President?"

Coordination tactics[a]

"When dealing with your Senator and/or staff, did the White House . . .
  ". . . consult your Senator to help effectively use policy information and
    analysis in Congress?"
  ". . . consult your Senator to help devise, develop, and execute the White
    House's legislative strategy?"

[a] Asked about the White House's effort exerted on their senator, respondents answered
"none at all" (0), "a little effort" (1), or "a lot of effort" (2) for each activity. Respective
items were averaged to create "bargaining" and "coordination" indexes, scaled from
0 to 2.

3.3.3.3 Measuring White House lobbying: "going public." To augment
this behind-the-scenes lobbying, I collected an additional piece of evidence: the locations of President Bush's going-public tax cut events.
My interviews indicated that these events were carefully considered
as an important part of the White House's lobbying operation, and
they were almost exclusively targeted at bolstering the president's
prospects in the Senate. Accordingly, I looked at each of President
Bush's public speeches between January 20 (inauguration day) and
June 8 (signing ceremony celebration), 2001, and coded a tax cut
event as one where at least 10 percent of the speech was devoted to
the issue of tax cuts. There were twenty-two such events held outside
Washington, D.C.

3.4   THE PATTERNS OF PRESIDENTIAL LOBBYING

Following Richard Neustadt's (1990[1960]) discerning lead, political scientists have largely agreed that, without any strong constitutional policymaking powers, presidential influence instead depends on an administration's ability to wield the informal resources at their disposal. And wield these resources they do. I found that the White House's offensive in promoting the president's tax cut bill included more than twenty thousand meetings with senators. It was, in Washington parlance, "the full-court press."

Figure 3.4 shows the sources who carried out the Bush administration's lobbying – the executers of those twenty thousand "touches" of U.S. senators. Not surprisingly, the Bush administration was truly that – an administration; the president himself was a participant in only 1 percent of the personal contacts with senators and/or their staffs. By and large, it was the president's surrogates who carried his case to Capitol Hill, led by White House staffers, augmented by political appointees inside the Treasury Department.

Although White House aides implemented most private lobbying, the president himself spearheaded the administration's public campaign. Augmenting the administration's personal conversations were more than sixty public events (including twenty-two outside the Beltway) held by President Bush. Figure 3.5 shows the states where the

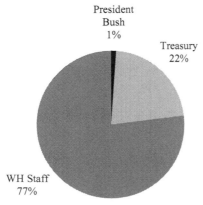

Figure 3.4 Sources of Administration's Lobbying Contacts, 2001 Tax Cut Debate.

States with Public
Tax Cut Event

Figure 3.5 Locations of President Bush's "Going-Public" Events, 2001 Tax Cut Debate.

president appeared at public events during the congressional debate over his tax cut plan.[15]

The important question for my purposes is, given these efforts, how should a strategic administration have targeted them? In contrast to the conception of White House coalition building in the Senate as being akin to "herding cats" one by one, I have predicted that only a handful of senators should be in the White House's lobbying crosshairs. The president and his team should focus their private meetings and public events at the president's leading allies, leading opponents, and potentially pivotal voters. Indeed, they should train their bargaining resources on the few leaders who will set the alternatives subject to vote and the few senators whose votes will decide which prevail. Additionally, the administration should work with its leading allies on how best to promote the president's bills.

A preliminary interrogation of these predictions, as in Table 3.5, corroborates them quite clearly. The White House's foremost Senate

[15] Not included in Figure 3.5 are Alaska and Hawaii, neither of which hosted a tax cut event with President Bush.

TABLE 3.5. *Targeting the president's lobbying offensive*

	Supportive leaders	Median voters	Opposing leaders	All others
Quantity of lobbying contacts (avg. no. of contacts per senator)[a]	5,847	70	359	17
Quality of lobbying contacts[a,b] (avg. per tactic, per senator)				
Bargaining	1.07	1.15	1.07	0.31
Coordination	1.83	0.50	0	0.32
"Going-public" events (avg. no. of events in state, per senator)	0.67	1.20	0.67	0.31

[a] Data are weighted to correct for oversample of leaders, committee members, and pivotal voters. Leaders include each party's two top floor leaders and committee leader; pivotal voters are the five senators closest to the fiftieth voter according to 2001 *Congressional Quarterly* Party Unity Scores.
[b] Asked about the White House's effort exerted on their senator for each activity, respondents answered "none at all" (0), "a little effort" (1), or "a lot of effort" (2).

lobbying targets were President Bush's leading allies. The supportive leaders had far more contact with the presidential advocates than did any other senators (including 350 times as many contacts as conducted with the average backbencher). And, as predicted, these meetings included a combination of bargaining and coordination, although there was particular emphasis on coordination. Indeed, the reason that White House officials and their leading legislative allies conversed so often was that they were, at several different levels, sharing policy information and updating political intelligence several times a day for months on end.

In addition to rallying their supportive leaders, the Bush administration also allocated immense resources to deterring leading opponents. Senate Democratic leaders were lobbied far more than other members and, in fact, averaged more than five times as many contacts as the Senate's five most pivotal voters. And, the nature of those interactions is telling. Rather than coordinating with opposing leaders on policy information or legislative options, the White House focused its efforts exclusively on changing these leaders' preferences. To be sure, leading opponents were barraged by the White House's persuasive arsenal, including President Bush's hosting a public rally in both the opposing committee's and the floor leader's home states. Speaking in South

Dakota, home of Minority Leader Tom Daschle (D-SD), the president reminded an excited crowd, "You're just an e-mail away from making a difference in somebody's attitude" (9 March 2001).

The final group predicted to be valuable lobbying targets is the one often highlighted in previous work – namely, pivotal voters. And, sure enough, the White House did channel substantial lobbying resources in these centrist senators' direction. Compared to other backbenchers, administration officials averaged fifty additional contacts with the Senate's likely swing voters. The thrust of these meetings was more bargaining than coordination, although there was some modest information sharing between administration and potentially pivotal voters. Perhaps most noteworthy, however, is the White House's disproportionate going-public effort aimed at the Senate's median voters. The president averaged more than one tax cut event in each swing senator's home state. Even though these events typically occurred in different cities on the same day, this still reflects a substantial allocation of the president's time and energy.

All told, the descriptive patterns of presidential lobbying seen in the 2001 tax cut traced closely the theorized tenets of agenda-centered and vote-centered lobbying. Not only did the White House lobby the predicted senators in the predicted ways: they seemed to do little else. Of the White House's contacts with senators on Capitol Hill, more than 95 percent occurred with the six leaders and five most pivotal voters. Likewise, "none at all" was the median response among nonleading, nonpivotal senators across *all* twelve tactics measured.

Of course, inferences based on descriptive analyses are tenuous; uncertainty and/or alternative explanations often lead to erroneous inferences. So, despite finding substantial support through this first cut at the data, further inquiry is needed. To better test the two-pronged theory of presidential lobbying, let me now revisit these analyses using more rigorous methods.

3.4.1 Testing White House Lobbying: Quantity

Translating the theoretical model into a statistical model, the multiple regression that follows includes two variables that test the agenda-centered strategy: one dummy variable for the president's leading allies, one for his leading opponents. In both instances, the leaders included are each side's respective leader on the Finance Committee, along with their top two floor leaders (e.g., the majority/minority leader and the whip). To isolate the importance of leadership posts, which I argue make these leaders the key players in congressional agenda setting, I also control for each senator's partisanship as well as whether or not he or she was on the committee of jurisdiction. Inclusion of these dummy variables means that the leading ally and leading opponent estimates reflect only the lobbying increases associated with holding a leadership post, independent of the senator's partisanship and committee membership.

Accounting for the vote-centered portion of the theory are the model's final two variables. The first is a dummy variable for the five senators closest to the median according to the 2001 *CQ* Party Unity Scores; the second interacts this initial measure of "pivotal voters" with committee membership, thereby testing the hypothesis that it is not just pivotal voters that are decisive but especially pivotal voters on the committee of jurisdiction (because of the cues they send to like-minded colleagues) (see Krehbiel 1991). Together, these variables appraise whether the White House disproportionately lobbied the Senate's swing voters, all else being equal.[16]

As the final point, recall that the dependent variable here is an interval-level estimate of "the number of conversations – face-to-face or on the phone – that [each] Senator and his/her staff had with the following people," which includes the administration officials who had advocated the president's case on Capitol Hill.[17]

Table 3.6 indicates the multiple regression results regarding the White House's lobbying contacts with senators and their staffs. The findings mirror the descriptive results. They show that when pressing

[16] Again, the agenda-centered and vote-centered strategies are not mutually exclusive; in fact, the latter can be employed to bolster the former. However, because the coefficients for pivotal voters are observationally equivalent, it is impossible to partition how much of the lobbying aimed at pivots was for their votes per se and how much was actually intended to "soften" leading opponents' leverage in negotiations. Instead, these tests only allow me to say whether or not senators' proximity to the "pivot point" made them especially lucrative lobbying targets.

[17] Because this dependent variable is an event-count measure – i.e., a count of the number of lobbying contacts between the administration and each senator – ordinary least-squares regression cannot be used. Instead, the proper estimating technique is a negative binomial regression (see Long 1997).

TABLE 3.6. *Negative binomial regression: quantity of White House lobbying*

	Coefficient (SE)	z-score
Leading ally	4.83 (1.23)	3.92**
Leading opponent	3.43 (1.35)	2.54**
Median voter * Committee member	−.19 (1.85)	−.10
Median voter, floor	2.39 (1.14)	2.09**
Committee member	.79 (.76)	1.04
President's party	1.40 (.62)	2.25**
Constant	1.66 (.40)	4.13**
log likelihood	−212.41	
N	55	

Note: SE, standard error. Dependent variable: interval-level estimate of the number of contacts between administration officials and each senator's office. ** $p < .05$ (two-tailed).

President Bush's tax cut case on Capitol Hill, White House lobbyists sought out leading allies, leading opponents, and pivotal voters. All else being equal, for every meeting between the administration and an average nonpivotal backbencher, leading allies are expected to receive 250 more, while leading opponents and pivotal voters are predicted to receive 15 and 11 times more, lobbying contacts than their backbencher colleagues.

Because these estimates arise from just one case (with one president, in one chamber), the exact numbers cited are not especially meaningful. That is, they do not suggest the exact lobbying patterns we should find elsewhere. Instead, what they do show is that for this crucial test of presidential lobbying in an important, controversial public policy debate, the White House's focus on the three predicted groups of senators is substantively noteworthy and statistically reliable. Thus, the observed lobbying patterns corroborate the thesis that the White House executed agenda-centered and vote-centered strategies to promote President Bush's tax cut plan in the Senate.

3.4.2 Testing White House Lobbying: Quality

Turning to the nature of the presidential–congressional interactions, Table 3.7 reports an investigation of the administration's choice of bargaining and coordination tactics. Because the logic predicting presidential lobbying targets is the same logic that predicts presidential

TABLE 3.7. *Ordinary least-squares regression: quality of White House lobbying*

	Bargaining		Coordination	
	Coefficient (SE)	t	Coefficient (SE)	t
Leading ally	.61 (.27)	2.27**	1.00 (.37)	2.72**
Leading opponent	.73 (.25)	2.90**	−.22 (.35)	−.65
Median voter *				
Committee member	−.21 (.39)	−.53	.69 (.54)	1.29
Median voter, floor	.83 (.24)	3.45**	−.02 (.33)	−.06
Committee member	.18 (.14)	1.31	.31 (.19)	1.62
President's party	.16 (.12)	1.41	.50 (.16)	3.18**
Constant	.21 (.09)	2.49**	.02 (.12)	.16
R^2	.44		.37	
N	55		55	

Note: SE, standard error. Dependent variables: For various "types of interactions" listed, senate staffers indicated the effort the White House had exerted on their office in that regard: none at all (0), a little effort (1), or a lot of effort (2). The relevant activities were sorted into a "bargaining" index and a "coordination" index, scaled from 0 to 2. ** $p < .05$ (two-tailed).

lobbying tactics, I use the same statistical model as in the preceding section.

As before, the empirical results nicely fit the theoretical predictions. When targeting legislators with the White House's bargaining arsenal, President Bush's aides disproportionately sought out leading allies, leading opponents, and pivotal voters (again, with pivotal voters on the Finance Committee receiving no more bargaining attention than those not on the Committee). Compared to the average (nonpivotal) backbencher (who can expect "a little" effort on three of the ten bargaining tactics measured), the White House is predicted to exert three times as much effort bargaining with leading allies and leading opponents and four times as much effort bargaining with the most likely swing voters.

In comparison to the administration's choice of bargaining targets, decisions regarding with whom to coordinate appear to be far more restrictive. It seems that the White House team only consistently shared information with their fellow partisans, and even among that group of supporters, the vast majority of the effort was aimed at its leaders. In fact, leading allies are the only ones predicted to partake in more than "a little" coordination with presidential staffers. These results, therefore, strongly corroborate the thesis that the White House's best options in this case entailed lobbying congressional leaders and pivotal voters, making each more sympathetic to the president's wishes, while coordinating with leading allies to harvest the fruits of that bargaining labor.

3.4.3 Testing White House Lobbying: "Going Public"

My final test of the White House's lobbying operation is somewhat different. Rather than look at the behind-the-scenes lobbying across Pennsylvania Avenue, here I examine the president's persuasive efforts outside the Beltway. As noted earlier, administration officials viewed this as an important component of their lobbying enterprise, which they directed almost exclusively to helping prevail in the Senate. As such, I predict that these decisions should correspond to my bargaining predictions. After all, my view of going public is that it is one element in a more general class of bargaining tactics.

That being said, several factors complicate testing the White House's going public lobbying efforts. Foremost among these challenges is that going-public events, although targeted at particular members, are implemented at particular locations. This causes difficulties because there is not a one-to-one correspondence between legislator and location (e.g., there are two senators from each state locale), which means that going-public events hit not only their intended target but also other members.

Because public lobbying events, unlike private lobbying, hit multiple targets at once, properly sorting intended and unintended targets requires an approach different from that used in the preceding section. Ultimately, I realized that this meant testing the locations where President Bush held his going-public rallies, not the senators who were subject to them: for if my predictions are right – some senators are the real targets of the event, others merely collateral damage – then areas that are home to leading allies, leading opponents, and pivotal voters should prove particularly lucrative choices for a going-public event, all else being equal.

TABLE 3.8. *Probit regression: location of President Bush's "going-public" events*

	Coefficient (robust SE)[a]	z-score
Leading ally	.51 (.30)	1.70*
Leading opponent	1.09 (.31)	3.52**
Median voter * Committee member	.07 (.08)	.98
Median voter, floor	.88 (.24)	3.73**
Natural log no. of Bush votes	.44 (.09)	4.87**
"Battleground" state, 2000	.34 (.19)	1.74*
Virginia	.84 (.22)	3.86**
Texas	.13 (.15)	.86
Constant	−7.05 (1.04)	−6.79**
log likelihood	−102.17	
N	3,116	

Note: Dependent variable: whether President Bush held a tax cut event in each county (1) or not (0). Standard errors (SE) are adjusted for clustering on state. $*p < .10; **p < .05$ (two-tailed).

Here I execute such a test by examining which counties the White House targeted for going-public tax cut rallies.[18] In addition to variables identifying whether the county was from one of the expected lobbying targets – homes of leading allies, leading opponents, or swing senators – several control variables are included in the model. The first indicates whether the state was an electoral battleground in the 2000 election (i.e., the state's winning margin for president was less than 3 percentage points). I also include dummy variables for Virginia and Texas, the former because of its proximity to Washington, D.C., and the latter because it is President Bush's home state.[19] Finally, I account for the potential that President Bush's public events were really aimed at rallying supporters per se (rather than persuading senators) by controlling for the natural log of President Bush's vote total in each county in the 2000 election.

As detailed in Table 3.8, the White House's going-public choices show patterns similar to those seen in private lobbying. Beyond eyeing

[18] These data were collected for a different study that examines, in detail, the geography and constituency motivations behind going-public events. This is why the unit of analysis is the county (rather than the state or congressional district).

[19] I would have also included a dummy variable for Maryland (which also borders the national capital), but because President Bush did not have any public tax cut events there, it was dropped from the analyses.

states that were geographically close or electorally crucial, the president's advisors further sought out states home to the Senate's leading allies, leading opponents, and swing voters. The latter two groups, in particular, were likely to experience a public rally hosted by the president in support of his agenda. Beyond that, the president's team also preferred to visit counties filled with like-minded voters.[20] All else being equal, the predicted probability of a presidential tax cut event in a large, supportive county was 42 percent for leading allies, 87 percent for leading opponents, and 72 percent for swing voters.

It is worth noting that these findings contradict the notion that going public is incompatible with bargaining. Instead, I find that the White House's inside and outside lobbying efforts are complementary; they both fit within the class of bargaining tactics that modern administrations can use to help mobilize leading allies, deter leading opponents, and attract pivotal voters. And that is exactly how President Bush and his aides deployed them. The question left begging, of course, is, did they work?

3.5 ASSESSING THE OUTCOME

Having now seen that the White House's tactical choices throughout the 2001 Senate tax cut debate fit the precepts of agenda-centered and vote-centered lobbying, the *process* of presidential coalition building looks as expected. Still unclear, however, is whether the *outcome* does as well. While my argument portrays the White House as influencing leaders' alternatives in the legislative earlygame to circumvent pivotal voters' preferences in its endgame, the opposite could be true. That is, it could happen that earlygame interactions prove irrelevant and/or unimportant. This would be the case if leaders merely served as proxies for pivotal voters or, alternatively, if the White House's interactions with pivotal voters, although far fewer in number, ultimately proved decisive. Properly testing this theory, therefore, requires pushing this study one step farther, from assessing the process to assessing its outcome.

---

[20] Including a variable for the county's overall population does not change the results as presented. It is neither substantively nor statistically significant.

Unfortunately, as with *ex ante* status quos discussed previously, measuring *ex post* policy outcomes is not straightforward. Here again, there exists no viable standard for appraising a new law's ideological content. Luckily, my task here is made somewhat easier because the crucial test is not the outcome's content per se but rather whether the bill President George W. Bush signed into law largely reflected swing senators' "ideal." If so, my insistence that the congressional endgame depends, in part, on what happens during the earlygame would be far less convincing. This is particularly true for the 2001 Senate tax cut debate, where I argued agenda-centered lobbying is likely to be applicable and efficacious.

To test whether pivotal voters' preferences ultimately prevailed (thereby obviating the earlygame's importance), I had the five most median senators' top tax aides evaluate provisions of the first Bush tax cuts as ultimately passed in the Senate. To do so, I broke the bill into its five basic domains: general tax provisions, child-related provisions, education-related provisions, retirement-related provisions, and estate/inheritance-related provisions. For each, I asked the pivotal senators' tax staffers to indicate, "If your boss could have unilaterally changed the bill that ultimately passed, what kinds of changes would he or she have made: no changes, minor changes, significant changes, or drastic changes?" Additionally, I said, "Or, if you didn't follow that particular issue closely enough to make a judgment, just indicate that you cannot say." Upon reading the question, I handed each respondent a form listing the provisions and all possible answers (including "cannot say"). They checked off their answers.

Table 3.9 reports how the Senate's five pivotal voters' appraised their chamber's tax cut product. These results reveal that centrists were far from content with many of the final bill's provisions. On the most important provisions – the general tax provisions – none said that they would make no changes; a plurality said that they would make "significant changes." Also, note that on the estate tax provisions, which reflect a top priority of the White House and their allies, all five of these swing senators would have made at least significant changes to the provisions that ultimately passed. Interestingly, I gave this same form to three senior officials from President Bush's administration, who each answered that the president would have made only "minor

TABLE 3.9. *Five median senators' assessment of the tax cut as signed into law*

Provisions	No changes	Minor changes	Significant changes	Drastic changes	Cannot say
General tax	0	1	3	1	0
Child tax related	1	3	0	0	1
Education tax related	0	1	1	0	3
Retirement tax related	0	3	0	0	2
Estate tax related	0	0	4	1	0

Note: Considered under budget reconciliation rules, the Senate decided the tax cut debate by simple majority rule, meaning that the pivotal voter was the median. To capture the senators most likely to cast the pivotal vote, therefore, I used the five senators nearest the median according to 2001 *CQ* Party Unity Scores.

changes" across all five areas. Hence, it appears that the White House ended up being more satisfied with the outcome than any of the pivotal voters were.

These findings are hardly novel to close congressional observers, and they were clear even before floor roll-call votes were cast. In fact, whereupon the bill finally reached the Senate floor and ostensibly became open to amendments, *The New York Times* reported that, despite the potential for changes, "It was clear from the outset that all these amendments would be rejected, [which] explained why the debate on them lacked passion" (22 May 2001).[21] And, indeed, when the bill and conference report were passed a week later, the prevailing wisdom concluded that President Bush had gotten most of what he wanted. The American Enterprise Institute's John Fortier and Norman Ornstein (2003, 151) concluded, "In a substantive sense, the president had a huge victory. The tax cut that was enacted into law was more than 80% of the size he proposed and much larger than

[21] Supporting the claim that endgame drama was dampened because of earlygame deal making was the ire liberal commentators directed at the Democratic leader on the Finance Committee, Senator Max Baucus (D-MT). In an article entitled "Bad Max," Matthew Yglesias wrote, "During the 2001 tax-cut debate, Baucus cut a deal with committee Chairman Chuck Grassley (R-IA) and the White House to co-sponsor a slightly watered-down version of the president's proposal. In doing so, he not only gave the GOP his vote but, more importantly, his support for the tax cut effectively handed the White House the staff and other committee resources under his control" (*American Prospect*, 1 February 2004, 11–13).

Democrats had wanted. Most of the details resembled the president's original plan" (see also Hacker and Pierson 2006).

3.6 CONCLUSION

In planning and in execution, every White House lobbying operation looks to exploit the legislative process to the president's advantage. As I tell it, the nature of this strategic legislative work entails lobbying each side's leaders (to manipulate the policy alternatives reaching the floor) and potentially pivotal voters (to influence which among those alternatives ultimately prevails). This chapter has tested these predictions with an array of in-depth evidence on presidential–congressional interactions during the 2001 tax cut debate in the U.S. Senate. I have also offered modest evidence regarding the effectiveness of the White House's efforts.

The first set of analyses examined the practices of presidential lobbying. Specifically, looking at the Bush administration's choice of lobbying targets and tactics in support of his preferred bill, I showed that the White House did systematically lobby leading allies, leading opponents, and swing voters. In fact, further tests confirmed that the president's advocates disproportionately targeted all three key Senate constellations with the White House's bargaining arsenal, while simultaneously coordinating with their leading allies to capitalize on any support the president's team could muster. All told, these results strongly corroborate the idea that White House officials, when heading to Capitol Hill, not only perceive the policymaking potential in agenda-centered and vote-centered strategies but also work hard to capitalize on it with their lobbying.

Finding empirical support for the practices of presidential lobbying, I then turned to evidence regarding their effectiveness. As explained previously, the question still begging was whether the White House's lobbying served to circumvent pivotal voters' preferences (as I argued) or merely to satisfy them (as straight voting models would suggest). In investigating this claim, I asked both swing senators and White House officials to appraise the overall outcome of the 2001 tax cut debate, with interesting results: while several White House officials indicated that they would have made only "minor" changes to the bill President

Bush signed into law, the Senate's most centrist members indicated that, if possible, each would have made "significant" changes to key provisions. At the very least, these results offer compelling evidence that the White House did not feel the president had capitulated to swing senators' wishes, and swing senators did not feel they had effectively determined the new law.

Having emphasized the strength of these analyses and the clarity of the findings, it is also important to recognize their limits, which all arise from one basic fact: while I made the decision to study the Bush administration's efforts to promote tax cut legislation in the 107th Senate precisely because this situation was typical of many major, controversial legislative debates, it is indeed just one case – with just one bill, one administration, and one chamber of Congress. Therefore, my conclusions are necessarily tentative and my extrapolations necessarily tenuous.

However, what new findings beg for is further study, and the results presented in this chapter certainly fit that mold. Indeed, as we have seen that agenda-centered and vote-centered lobbying do occur, there is good reason to believe that tracing the implications further will elucidate the processes and products of presidential–congressional interactions. The next two chapters seek to do just that.

CHAPTER FOUR

Winning Key Votes, 1953–2004

Whether it is President Lyndon Johnson calling Senator Abraham Ribicoff (D-CT) – "He told me what a low-life bastard I was and how I'd better get right with God" (*Time*, 7 August 1978) – or President Bill Clinton calling Senator Bob Kerrey (D-NE) – "If you want to bring this presidency down, then go ahead" (Stephanopoulos 1999, 176) – tales of presidents' pleas for lawmakers' support before crucial roll-call votes still reverberate across Washington. On both ends of Pennsylvania Avenue, these and comparable anecdotes are often said to reveal the essence of presidential power and exemplify its exertion on Capitol Hill. As John F. Kennedy noted, "The President must initiate policies and devise laws to meet the needs of the Nation. And he must be prepared to use all the resources of his office to . . . not let down those supporting his views on the floor" (17 January 1960).

But, of course, popular imagery of presidential power is one thing; systematic evidence is quite another. And by the latter standard, presidents' chances of securing legislative success have been appraised at less than the advertised value. Across various types of floor votes, including the most important ones, each president's fate has appeared to be largely (if not wholly) preset by the congressional delegation he confronts. For example, after accounting for a chamber's basic composition, seemingly "skilled" presidents (e.g., Lyndon Johnson) experience success and failure rates comparable to those of their reputedly "unskilled" colleagues (e.g., Jimmy Carter), leading many to infer that presidential success or failure has little to do with the president.

To illustrate this basic conclusion, Figure 4.1 displays each president's success in *CQ* "key" House votes and the percentage of the

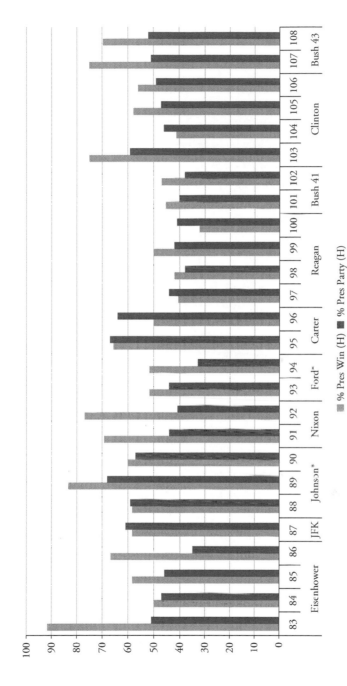

Figure 4.1 Presidential Party's Percentage of Members and "Key" Vote Wins: House of Representatives (H).
Note: *For the 88th and 93rd Congresses, Presidents Johnson and Ford actually finished the terms begun under their predecessors.

chamber held by his fellow partisans, from 1953 to 2004. As the figure demonstrates, Lyndon Johnson and Jimmy Carter both faced similar House delegations and secured similar levels of success on key
roll-call votes. In fact, President Carter (1995) cited the similarity to
refute charges of his ineffectiveness. He wrote, "In spite of my having
to face with them some extremely controversial subjects, *Congressional
Quarterly* magazine found that during my four years in office I won
approximately three out of four roll-call votes on issues on which I
had taken a clear position.... Lyndon Johnson, the masterful congressional manipulator, had a support score that was only a little higher –
82 percent" (93).

The more general point holds as well: presidents' success in key votes
moves largely in tandem with congressional predispositions. Those
presidents fortunate enough to inherit a legislature filled with like-
minded lawmakers typically find success in floor votes; those facing
a Congress composed of oppositional lawmakers do not. The same
general pattern also fits the Senate, as shown in Figure 4.2.

As conclusive as these results appear at first blush, I theorized
that they miss essential elements of presidents' success, let alone
influence. One reason is that the relevant comparison is not across
presidents (e.g., skilled versus unskilled) but rather across bills (i.e.,
lobbied versus not). Also, because endgame success often depends
on earlygame influence, I argue that one cannot accurately assess the
former without recognizing the latter. And, indeed, by accounting for
prevoting and voting processes, this chapter sheds new light on the
mechanisms of presidential coalition building and, more important,
their effectiveness.

4.1   INCORPORATING THE EARLYGAME

Before hosting a highly coveted signing ceremony, a president must
first get a legislative initiative past two thresholds: he must (1) reach
a roll-call vote, and (2) prevail in that vote. Looking only at the
latter stage – that is, the endgame voting stage – thus offers a distorted view of policymaking, as it omits the many proposals that could
have made it to a vote but did not. This omission is especially pertinent if, as I argue, presidents can manipulate upstream processes to

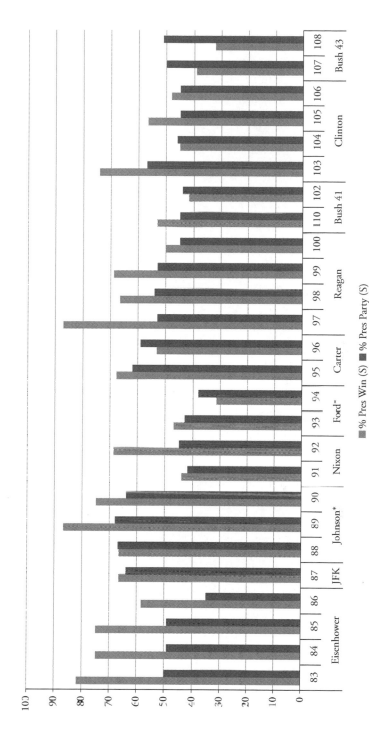

Figure 4.2 Presidential Party's Percentage of Members and "Key" Vote Wins: Senate (S).

Note: *For the 88th and 93rd Congresses, Presidents Johnson and Ford actually finished the terms begun under their predecessors.

■ % Pres Win (S)   ■ % Pres Party (S)

influence downstream outcomes. Rather than analyzing presidential success or failure in votes in isolation, therefore, a better approach would account for prevoting processes as well. Put differently, properly assessing presidents' legislative impact on roll-call votes requires appraising the vote's outcome *given that the issue got to a vote.*

The study summarized here and detailed in the Appendix sought to account for presidential–congressional interactions across the entire legislative process. Specifically, I started the process by drawing from the Policy Agendas Project (www.policyagendas.org) comprehensive taxonomy in *CQ Almanac.* Focusing on seven major domestic policy domains – civil rights, community and housing, education, energy, health, social welfare, and taxes – and fifty-five corresponding subtopics for every Congress between the 83rd (1953–54) and the 108th (2003–4), a systematic culling from the Policy Agendas dataset identified 769 relevant policy initiatives. For each, a research team coded the White House's involvement along with numerous other variables, including the results of any corresponding *CQ* "key" votes. The upshot: the dataset gathered to test the effectiveness of presidents' lobbying includes 769 major domestic legislative initiatives, 113 key House votes, and 100 key Senate votes for the period spanning 1953–2004.

It is worth reiterating that this new approach allows unprecedented tests of presidents' influence on roll-call votes. By measuring presidents' lobbying and accounting for the entire legislative process, I can simultaneously investigate the effectiveness of presidential coalition building in the earlygame *and* the endgame, accounting for the relationship between the two (all else being equal). Let me now turn to just such a test.

4.2 THE (UNRELENTING) PRESIDENTIAL PUSH

That contemporary Americans expect their chief executives to play a key legislative role is clear, as is the fact that today's presidents make extraordinary efforts to meet that expectation. Indeed, modern presidents routinely comment on, and lobby for, policy positions they support.

Table 4.1 reports the extent of presidents' involvement in domestic lawmaking from Dwight Eisenhower's tenure through the first

TABLE 4.1. *President's involvement in U.S. lawmaking, 1953–2004[a]*

	Avg. no. domestic initiatives per Congress during each administration	Of issues considered, percentage where president[b]		
		Played no role	Endorsed a position	Actively lobbied
Eisenhower	17	19%	21%	60%
Kennedy	33	15%	42%	42%
Johnson	30	13%	28%	58%
Nixon	38	38%	26%	36%
Ford	40	25%	38%	38%
Carter	37	26%	15%	59%
Reagan	38	42%	18%	40%
Bush (41)	38	43%	7%	50%
Clinton	24	39%	15%	45%
Bush (43)	15	21%	34%	45%
Mean	31	28%	24%	47%
(SD)	(9.3)	(11.5)	(11.4)	(9.2)

[a] Excludes Congresses where the presidency switched hands – i.e., the Eighty-Eighth (Kennedy to Johnson) and Ninety-Third (Nixon to Ford). Also, data for President George W. Bush (43) are limited to his first term.

[b] The president's involvement was determined through a content analysis of each bill's coverage in *CQ Almanac*. Research assistants agreed on presidents' role in 93.5% of the double-coded cases ($n = 249$).

term of George W. Bush, 1953–2004. Among issues receiving serious congressional consideration, presidents have spoken or lobbied in support of a preferred position on nearly three-quarters of them, with no president sitting out more than 43 percent of domestic issues.

Looking at the patterns more closely, one important point emerges: presidents' legislative involvement does not vary much by the Congress they happen to confront. That is to say, it does not look like presidents strategically tailor their efforts because they want to experience success or avoid failure per se but rather because they want to achieve more existential goals like implementing good policy and/or satisfying campaign promises. Of course, many previous scholars have noted as much. Paul Light (1999) found that presidents' legislative agenda push for issues based on their electoral and policy goals, then compromise in light of congressional realities. Mark Peterson (1990) agreed, finding: "It seems fairly certain that the strategic-accommodation scenario – leading to the notion that the president's program is a hopeless muddle – can be pretty well laid to rest" (66; see also Fett 1994).

TABLE 4.2 *Correlations of president's involvement in U.S. lawmaking, 1953–2004*

Congressional factor	Correlation with president's involvement
Divided government	
House	−.09
Senate	−.05
President to median: House	−.07
President to filibuster pivot: Senate	−.05
Environmental factors	
Positive exogenous events	−.03
Negative exogenous events	.06
Vietnam War	.10
Cold War period	.00
Iraq War I	−.09
9/11 attack/Afghanistan	.02
Iraq War II	−.01
Presidential factors	
Honeymoon period	.00
Lame duck period	−.03
Tenure	−.02
President's political capital	.01

Note: Dependent variable: the president's involvement was determined through a content analysis of each bill's coverage in *Congressional Quarterly Almanac*. It is coded as played no role (0), endorsed a position (1), or actively lobbied (2). Testing all these variables in the context of a multiple (ordered probit) regression yields an overall pseudo-$R^2 = .02$.

Even so, based on the idea that it is better to err on the side of caution, I still considered using a statistical model to account for the strategic aspects of presidents' lobbying. This seemed especially worthwhile as previous treatments were based less on systematic evidence than personal observation. As such, I sought out possible "instruments" correlated with presidential lobbying but not congressional success (except inasmuch as lobbying affects success).[1]

Table 4.2 reports the results of my attempt to find good instruments for presidential lobbying. Suffice it to say, none were found. In fact,

---

[1] If an independent variable is correlated with the model's errors (as would be the case here if presidents strategically adapted their lobbying to inflate their successes and mask their failures), replacing that variable with good "instruments" in the context of a two-stage least squares (2SLS) regression can help circumvent the problem (see Greene 2007; Long 1997). However, this benefit is realized only inasmuch as the instruments are "good," as defined in the text.

these results strongly corroborate the prevailing wisdom that contemporary presidents have actively involved themselves in lawmaking on domestic issues, largely without concern for the obstacles their positions confront on Capitol Hill. An administration's domestic lobbying does not ebb in the face of a hostile Congress, because of a full plate elsewhere, or when political fortunes fade, nor does it flow in more favorable circumstances. Actually, none of the variables listed is even moderately correlated with presidents' lobbying, and putting them all together to predict presidents' involvement (in the context of a multiple ordered probit regression) yields the paltry pseudo-R^2 value of .02. The upshot: if, all else being equal, we find that presidents' lobbying increases their prospects for legislative success, there is no reason to think that this relationship reflects presidents "jumping in front of the congressional parade" rather than actually influencing lawmakers and legislation.

4.3 REACHING AND WINNING KEY VOTES

Obviously, attempting influence is one thing; exerting it, quite another. Having just examined the former, now I can probe the latter. Are presidents' extensive efforts aimed at influencing lawmakers effective, or are presidents merely tilting at windmills? In this section, I interrogate one important aspect of presidents' legislative potential by focusing on their ability to win key House and Senate roll-call votes. (In Chapter 5, I turn to assessing presidential influence on the overall outcome.)

As noted previously, one way that political scientists have tested presidents' potential influence is to compare their records on roll-call votes that *CQ* flags as "key" because they comprise "a matter of major controversy, a test of presidential or political power, and a decision of potentially great impact on the nation and on lives of Americans" (*CQ Weekly*, 1 January 2007, 60). Figure 4.3 offers a somewhat different but comparable look; it displays presidents' overall success in key votes by the level of their involvement.

The results shown in Figure 4.3 suggest what similar studies (see esp. Bond and Fleisher 1990; Edwards 1989; Fleisher and Bond 2000) have suggested before: presidents seemingly have little effect on members' voting. The bivariate correlations between presidential lobbying and

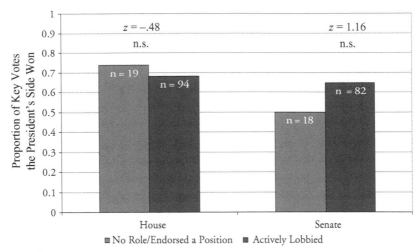

Figure 4.3 Presidential Success in "Key" Domestic Votes, by the President's Involvement, 1953–2004.

key vote success are low in both cases and actually negative in the House (–.05 in the House, .12 in the Senate). Overall, this (floor-only) analysis suggests that presidents' lobbying does not significantly change their chances for winning key votes ($p = .63$ in the House, $p = .28$ in the Senate).

That said, the caveat I have emphasized time and again is that votes generally, and key votes in particular, comprise only a limited portion of the legislative process, for a small subset of bills seriously considered. That would be fine if they still offered a representative picture. However, if my theory is right – that is, if presidents' influence often works by affecting what makes it to a vote, not necessarily by affecting what wins once there – then tests based exclusively on votes have missed an important aspect of president-led coalition building and underplayed a substantial portion of their success. Indeed, presidential success may occasionally require winning knock-down, drag-out floor fights – but not always and perhaps not even typically.

A first cut at the data underscores this point. Although the bivariate correlations between White House involvement and *winning* key votes are low, the relationships between White House involvement and *reaching* key votes are not ($r = .30$ in the House, $r = .29$ in the Senate).

The obvious question left begging is whether the latter (reaching key votes) has implications for the former (winning them). I consider the answer in section 4.3.1.

4.3.1   A Multiple Regression Test

To account more systematically for the relationship between prevoting and voting stages in Congress, and particularly presidents' role therein, the best approach tests presidents' success in key votes *given the factors that got them to key votes*. Fortunately, a selection model allows us to do just this by simultaneously testing the factors that affect the outcome of a key congressional vote along with the earlygame factors that led that particular initiative to a key vote in that particular Congress (see Greene 2007; Long 1997). Accordingly, the results that follow come from a selection model in which the dependent variable for the outcome (endgame) stage is 1 if the president's side prevailed and 0 if it did not, and the dependent variable for the selection (earlygame) stage is 1 if there was a key vote on the issue and 0 if there was not.

4.3.1.1 Endgame variables. Among the factors theorized to shape presidents' fate in the legislative endgame, especially on key votes, congressional predispositions are the most important. In particular, a central point in previous work (and incorporated in my model) highlights pivotal voters' decisive role in vote outcomes. The first endgame variable, therefore, notes the pivotal voter's ideological predisposition in each chamber. This means the median voter in the House of Representatives and the filibuster pivot in the Senate. Overall, the pivotal voters most predisposed to support a president served in the 95th Congress (Carter in 1977–78); those most predisposed to oppose a president served in the 104th (Clinton in 1995–96).

To examine the effectiveness of presidents' lobbying, the next variable included in the endgame model accounts for presidents' involvement, which, at this stage, largely reflects a vote-centered strategy aimed at pulling pivotal voters toward the president's position. As detailed in the Appendix, presidents' involvement was determined through a content analysis of *CQ Almanac*'s legislative summary for each bill. It is coded "played no role" (0), "endorsed a position" (1), and "actively lobbied" (2).[2]

The final important element in my stylized legislative endgame is presidents' "political capital" – a president's supply of bargaining resources or, behaviorally equivalent, lawmakers' receptivity to the president's appeals. Two of the more important factors underlying a president's political muscle are (1) his standing in the polls, and (2) the state of the national economy. Accordingly, a president's political capital is measured as a factor score of the president's yearly average presidential job approval (source: Gallup) and the nation's change in gross domestic product from the previous year (source: Bureau of Economic Analysis, U.S. Department of Commerce). To facilitate interpretation, this variable is cut into thirds, yielding a variable of presidential political capital that runs from 1 to 3, low to high. It is worth noting that although I consider this a political-environment variable because the president cannot significantly shape the national economy or public opinion, this does not render it unimportant for inferences about presidents' influence on Congress. Actually, the opposite is true; for things the president can control, political capital amplifies or diminishes his effectiveness.

To isolate tests of the previously theoretically derived variables, the outcome model also includes several political-environment variables as controls. These include secular trends long found to affect presidents' success in roll-call votes, including his honeymoon period (i.e., the first Congress he confronts), his lame duck period (i.e., the final Congress of a second term), and his overall tenure (i.e., the overall number of Congresses the president has faced).

4.3.1.2 *Earlygame variables.* Switching to the legislative earlygame, the selection portion of the model includes variables that predict which bills will even make it to a key vote. Again, the first and foremost of these indicate congressional predispositions, particularly congressional leaders' bargaining leverage. Accordingly, the selection model

---

[2] Research assistants agreed on presidents' role in 93.5% of the double-coded cases ($n = 249$).

indicates when a divided government reigned in a chamber during a particular Congress.

The second variable included in the selection model captures the impact of presidents' earlygame lobbying. It reflects my central thesis that beyond corralling support on the floor, much of presidential coalition building entails shaping the alternatives that make it to a vote. The central hypothesis, therefore, is not that presidents' lobbying increases the likelihood that a bill will experience a key vote but rather that White House officials wield that earlygame influence such that the president wins the key vote. Importantly, this prediction holds for presidential success in both the House and the Senate.

As before, I include several additional variables that help isolate tests of my core predictions. Most important among these control variables is a measure of each bill's salience, which tallies the coverage accorded each bill in the relevant *CQ Almanac* (in hundreds of words). Because salience is a function of controversy and importance, as well as the involvement of key players, this variable is critically important because it directly controls for issue-specific elements associated with presidential lobbying but conceptually distinct from it. I also include fixed-effects variables for each issue area (e.g., civil rights, education, and taxes) based on the idea that some issues are more likely to spawn key votes than others.

The final control variable in the selection model accounts for various events that can push domestic policy off the capital's front burner. Based on Lebo and Cassino's (2007) taxonomy of key events during presidents' terms, but excluding events related to domestic policy-making, this "exogenous events" measure counts the various real-world events that occurred during each Congress. The types of events included are wars (e.g., Desert Shield) and scandals (e.g., Monica Lewinsky), as well as moments that push foreign policy to the fore (e.g., bombing of Libya, Panama Canal Treaty). As with the other earlygame variables, this one tests which factors help push a domestic bill to a key vote or inhibit it from getting that far.

4.3.1.3 *Results.* As a reminder, I have theorized that the White House has two paths to legislative success: the first emphasizes pivotal voters in the legislative endgame; the second highlights congressional leaders in the legislative earlygame. And far from being mutually exclusive, these two lobbying strategies actually complement one another; the White House's ability to win an endgame floor fight bolsters its chances for striking a deal that obviates the need to do so.

Table 4.3 tests this theory using the selection model discussed earlier. The first noteworthy result is among the more subtle: tests show that accounting for what reaches a key vote does, in fact, have significant implications for what ultimately passes. In both the House ($\rho = -.44$, standard error [SE] $= .16$, $p < .05$) and the Senate ($\rho = -.45$, SE $= .22$, $p < .10$), the evidence indicates that analyzing key votes in isolation offers a distorted view; it underestimates presidential success in *CQ*'s key votes. Any number of potential explanations could account for this pattern – one is that *CQ* staffers are especially drawn to votes characterized by controversy and uncertainty, which means that they disproportionately overlook cases where presidents' earlygame lobbying proved effective – but the implication is the same regardless: in both chambers, the legislative endgame is inextricably tied to the earlygame, so properly appraising presidents' success in each requires accounting for both.

Because the evidence strongly corroborates the model's usefulness, I can now shift to answering this chapter's foremost question: Can a president influence, directly or indirectly, his success in key roll-call votes? To foreshadow, the answer is yes. Indeed, the clear finding from these analyses is that presidents' involvement – from playing no role, to endorsing a position, to actively lobbying – dramatically increases the likelihood that an issue will be subjected to a key vote, all else being equal. This is true in both the House ($b = .45$, SE $= .10$, $p < .05$) and the Senate ($b = .58$, SE $= .09$, $p < .05$) alike. More important, this ability to get provisions to a key vote in the earlygame helps presidents win those votes in the endgame *even if they cannot further enhance their success once an issue is on the floor.* Let me elaborate.

Because the results in Table 4.3 are maximum likelihood estimates, it is not easy to intuit their substantive meaning. To translate the findings more clearly, Figures 4.4 and 4.5 display the predicted probability that a president will reach and win or reach and lose a key vote versus the president's involvement, holding everything at its average (83rd

TABLE 4.3. *Multiple regression of presidents' success in* Congressional Quarterly's *key votes, 1953–2004*[a]

Model	House		Senate	
	Coefficient (robust SE)[b]	z-score	Coefficient (robust SE)[b]	z-score
Outcome				
President to pivotal voter	-.63 (1.12)	-.56	-2.95 (1.23)	-2.40**
White House involvement	-.37 (.24)	-1.58	.06 (.36)	.16
President's political capital	.20 (.17)	1.21	.10 (.15)	.67
Honeymoon period	.15 (.33)	.45	.31 (.34)	.90
Lame duck period	-.47 (.67)	-.70	-.13 (.55)	-.23
President's tenure	.06 (.26)	.24	-.02 (.19)	-.09
Constant	1.74 (1.30)	1.34	3.94 (1.72)	2.29**
Selection[c]				
Divided government	-.25 (.14)	-1.77*	.16 (.13)	1.25
White House involvement	.45 (.10)	4.51**	.58 (.09)	6.70**
Issue salience	.07 (.01)	6.03**	.07 (.01)	6.76**
Exogenous events	-.09 (.04)	-2.04**	-.02 (.04)	-.46
Constant	-1.82 (.33)	-5.54**	-2.65 (.29)	-9.09**
ρ	-.44 (.16)	-5.41**	-.45 (.22)	-3.09*
N	769 (656 censored)		769 (669 censored)	
log pseudolikelihood	-292.94		-253.22	

Note: *p < .10; **p < .05 (two-tailed).

[a] Results are derived from the simultaneous estimation of a selection model where a key vote's occurrence is the selection stage and its result is the outcome stage. Thus, the dependent variable for the earlygame is 1 if a bill had a key vote and 0 if it did not; the dependent variable for the endgame is 1 if the president's side prevailed and 0 if it did not.

[b] Standard errors (SE) are adjusted for clustering by each issue subtopic.

[c] The model also allows fixed effects for each major issue (e.g., civil rights, education, and taxes).

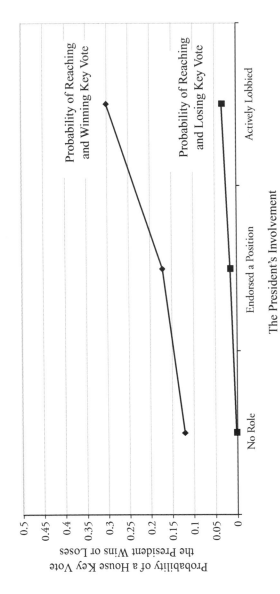

Figure 4.4 Predicted Probability of Winning and Losing "Key" Votes in the House, by the President's Involvement.

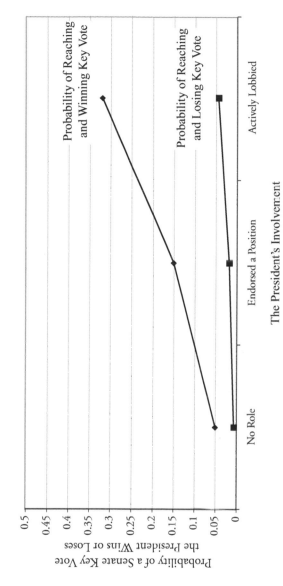

Figure 4.5 Predicted Probability of Winning and Losing "Key" Votes in the Senate, by the President's Involvement.

to 108th Congresses, 1953–2004) value, in the House and Senate, respectively.

Starting in the House of Representatives (Fig. 4.4), we see that a president's involvement helps him not only reach key votes but also win them. Absent any involvement, a president facing the average Congress in the average political environment will reach and win key votes on only 12 percent of the initiatives considered. However, this prospect increases dramatically as the president increases investments in promoting a preferred policy. On average, he will reach and win a key vote on 17 percent of the initiatives that he publicly endorses and 30 percent of those he actually supports with lobbying. By contrast, the probability that the president will reach and lose a key House vote is less than .05 in the average context and regardless of the president's legislative efforts.

The Senate results tell the same story, more emphatically (Fig. 4.5). A president's prospects for winning key votes in the upper chamber increase from .05 when he does nothing to .32 when he lobbies. Again, presidents' chances for losing key votes also increase with their involvement, but barely. Presidents who lobby will typically lose only one key vote for every twenty issues advocated.

Notably, while these findings affirm presidents' legislative impact on key votes even after controlling for the Congress and context they happen to inherit, as well as the significance of the issues they engage, this is not to say that Congress and context do not matter. In fact, these results affirm that their impact is substantial and potentially dispositive.

To show how extrapresidential factors condition presidents' effectiveness, now let me examine presidents' prospects for reaching and winning key votes under different conditions in the House and Senate, respectively. Specifically, I compare a president's chances for success, holding other values at equal levels, in two cases on opposite ends of my theory's opportunism spectrum: the Eighty-Ninth (1965–66) and Ninety-Fourth (1975–76) Congresses.[3] As Table 4.4 details, the former

---

3   However, all estimates hold the issue docket (e.g., health, civil rights, community, and housing) at the average mix for all postwar Congresses. This is important for isolating the impact of different congressional and political contexts independent of the issues each considered.

TABLE 4.4. *A tale of two Congresses (with the average in between)*

	The good: 89th Congress (1965–66)	The average	The bad: 94th Congress (1975–76)
President	Johnson		Ford
Presidential honeymoon (first Congress after newly elected president)	Yes	No	No
Presidential approval (Gallup, December before Congress)	69%	55%	42%
Change in gross domestic product (year before Congress)	5.8%	3.3%	−0.5%
President to pivotal voter (0–2, close– far)[a]			
House	0.85	1.02	1.19
Senate	1.09	1.18	1.35

[a] From DW-NOMINATE (www.voteview.com).

provided President Lyndon Johnson an especially advantageous setup, while the latter put President Gerald Ford in a particularly unfavorable situation. Mimicking the two thus provides useful archetypes for examining presidents' potential influence across a range of contexts – good to bad (and including the average).[4]

Examining Figures 4.6 and 4.7 reveals the conditional nature of presidential influence. For one, in certain circumstances, presidents are severely limited in their ability to win key votes. When, like President Gerald Ford, the president is endowed with little political capital and facing far-off pivotal voters (in both chambers), his prospects for reaching and winning key votes are grim. Lobbying certainly helps the president's probability of prevailing (from .08 to .21 in the House, from .03 to .20 in the Senate), but even then the odds are long.

[4] I use the particular values for these Congresses, except for the salience and type-of-issue variables, where I use the overall average for all cases. This allows me to isolate the impact of changes in congressional and contextual variables, independent of changes in the issues that are addressed by the president, the Congress, or both.

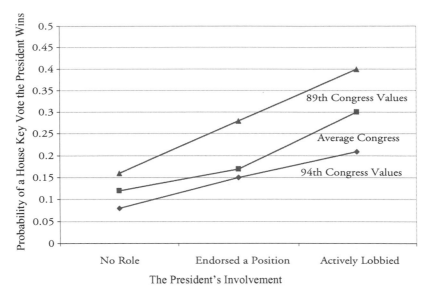

Figure 4.6 Predicted Probability of Reaching and Winning "Key" Votes: House.

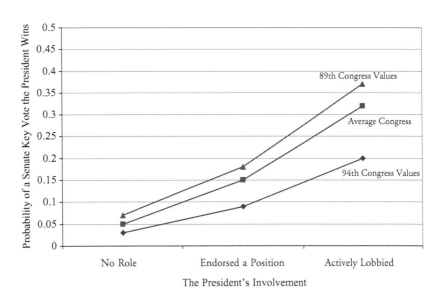

Figure 4.7 Predicted Probability of Reaching and Winning "Key" Votes: Senate.

By contrast, that same president's key vote outlook improves substantially if he is bequeathed a more agreeable congressional delegation, especially when backed by ample political capital. For these lucky presidents, like Lyndon Johnson in 1965, merely endorsing a bill can often result in its reaching and succeeding in a key vote (28 percent in the House, 17 percent in the Senate). And, of course, these prospects improve even further when such a favorably positioned president decides to actively lobby on behalf of a bill (an additional 12 and 19 percentage points in the House and Senate, respectively).

Given presidents' potential impact on Congress when they actively promote their preferred policies, it is worth recalling the extent of presidents' involvement in the postwar period. As detailed earlier in this chapter (see Table 4.1), contemporary presidents involve themselves in nearly three-fourths of the most important domestic issues considered during their terms. As such, these results affirm presidents' significant, if conditional, impact on the outcome of key roll-call votes, a legacy that extends beyond issuing vetoes or an idiosyncratic handful of headline-grabbing issues.

4.4 CONCLUSION

There are times when passing the president's agenda requires all-out lobbying just before key roll-call votes. Such moments provide great drama for those anxiously awaiting the result, as President Bill Clinton's team experienced while monitoring vote tallies on the president's first budget package:

> We watched the roll call in Clinton's study off the Oval. . . . I [George Stephanopoulos] was sitting in the leather desk chair. Clinton stood directly behind me, cigar clenched in his teeth, steadying himself like a captain on the bridge with his left hand on Mack [McLarty, Chief of Staff] and his right hand on me. I focused my energy on the little screen, trying to will the yeas up to 218. (Stephanopoulos 1999, 178)

When the yeas did finally reach that winning threshold, "the president's study erupted in a riot of hugs that soon subsided into sober relief" (179).

As memorable as moments like these are, they capture only a limited slice of national lawmaking, a small fraction of presidential–congressional interactions. As my theory has revealed, although lobbying pivotal voters to win roll-call votes is one path by which presidents can promote initiatives, it is not the only one; by lobbying congressional leaders, the White House can also manipulate the policy alternatives that make it that far. And, importantly, I have argued that these two strategies are related; a president's ability to change pivotal voters' preferences in the endgame casts the strategic shadow in which he negotiates a potential "deal" with opposing leaders before then.

Given these theoretical paths to presidential success, this chapter has more fully traced the empirical implications. What has emerged is a new blueprint for appraising presidents' potential impact on "key" roll-call votes. The most important insights hold that (1) a prerequisite to presidential influence is presidential involvement, and (2) properly testing presidential success in the endgame requires assessing his influence before then. This chapter has offered just such a test.

Examining the first point yielded several interesting insights about the nature of presidents' legislative involvement. For one, the results show that presidents have been active participants in the day's major legislative debates. Over the last half-century, presidents have publicly endorsed a preferred outcome on a quarter of issues and lobbied on behalf of another half. Partly because presidents have so frequently thrust themselves into the legislative process, the evidence further shows that presidents' lobbying is not tailored to maximize successes or minimize failures. Instead, presidents' push their agenda in good times and bad, early and late, and irrespective of the congressional lot they face. In short, I have shown that presidents frequently lobby for policies they want to see passed, regardless of how likely (or unlikely) that may be.

Given postwar presidents' extensive lobbying investments, the rest of the chapter examines their impact on key roll-call votes. With simultaneous testing of the earlygame factors that affect which bills experience key votes alongside the endgame factors that determine the winner, the results affirm that presidents' involvement does dramatically increase their chances of prevailing in key votes. However, the essence of this influence looks different than is often assumed. Rather than turning on their influence in the legislative endgame, presidents' success in key votes is rooted primarily in the earlygame. Again, this does not mean that the legislative endgame is unimportant or that presidents' vote-centered lobbying is irrelevant but rather underscores the fact that its impact typically works indirectly by affecting the bargaining that transpires before bills even reach the floor. This same pattern holds true in both chambers.

After the demonstration that presidents' efforts often prove to be effective, the chapter's final point offers the important caveat that this influence is not unconditional but rather interacts with the context and Congress each president happens to confront. When considering some major legislative issue, a president facing an agreeable lot in Congress can dramatically increase his chances of reaching and winning related key votes by lobbying on its behalf. Other presidents, by contrast, have fewer opportunities and less potential. For the president who inherits far-off pivotal voters and/or a divided government, advocating his agenda will certainly improve his chances of reaching and winning key votes, but that improvement will be only modestly effective, pushing his odds from none to slim.

CHAPTER FIVE

Signing New Laws, 1953–2004

Among the most highly prized tokens of legislative achievement are the pens presidents employ to seal it. Catering to the demand for so-called bill signers, presidents have found creative ways to increase the supply, from changing pens for each letter to adding various accents and squiggles. When President Kennedy found himself with more pens to use than letters left to write, he made up the difference by artistically underlining his signature. When President Reagan accidentally wrote two letters with one pen rather than the planned one-to-one ratio, he declared, "Oops, one letter too many. I'll have to catch up here someplace." Ultimately he did. After completing his signature, the president explained to an aide, "I figured how to do it. . . . I'll make one part of the 'n'" (13 August 1981).

Disjointed autographs notwithstanding, presidents' multiple-pen practice persists, and for good reason. As one article about John F. Kennedy's ballooning pen distribution noted, "It's a painless way to get on the good side of an important committee chairman, to give a lift to a supporter who's up for re-election or to recognize a friend in the other party. Who could do as much with a sword?" (*The New York Times*, 7 January 1962). At the same time, it is important to distinguish pens used to sign legislation from other White House trinkets. Lawmakers may certainly appreciate M&Ms, cufflinks, or playing cards emblazoned with the presidential seal, but none confuses those items with signing pens engraved simply but significantly "The President – the White House." The latter signify something more substantive: a change in public policy, sometimes a historic shift. Such was the case when President Lyndon Johnson signed into law the Civil Rights Act of 1964:

> With seventy-five pens, President Johnson signed the bill. He handed the first pen to [Senate Minority Leader] Everett Dirksen, the second to [Senate Democratic Whip] Hubert Humphrey, and others to [House Judiciary Chairman] Emanuel Celler and [House Judiciary Ranking Member] William McCulloch. He gave six pens to Robert Kennedy, recognizing the contributions of his Justice Department team. He handed pens to the leaders of the major civil rights organization, without whose efforts there would have been no law. Martin Luther King, Jr., Roy Wilkins, James Farmer, Whitney Young, and A. Philip Randolph each came forward to shake Johnson's hand and receive a pen. (Kotz 2005, 153)

Lyndon Johnson's signing the Civil Rights Act is an extreme example, to be sure, but legislative outcomes more generally have been at the heart of this book. I have argued that the focus of presidents' lobbying efforts, the essence of their legislative leadership, turns on what passes or does not. So having already examined presidents' lobbying choices and shown their effects on key roll-call votes, let me now turn to the most important test: whether presidents can influence what laws Congress passes (or does not).

5.1   THE PATTERNS OF PRESIDENTIAL SUCCESS

Frustrated by the capitol's slow pace as its August recess approached, President John Kennedy joked with reporters, "It is much easier in many ways for me, and for other Presidents, I think, who felt the same way, when Congress is not in town." After the laughter subsided, though, Kennedy's pragmatic view returned: "We ought to all stay here. . . . I think that we've got a number of things left to do and I am confident the Congress will stay and try to do them" (27 June 1962). President Kennedy's comments capture a typical sentiment. While presidents, even in favorable circumstances, find lawmakers slow to act and hard to direct, officials at both ends of Pennsylvania Avenue tend to keep trying. What's more, the capital's key players often find a way to get something done.

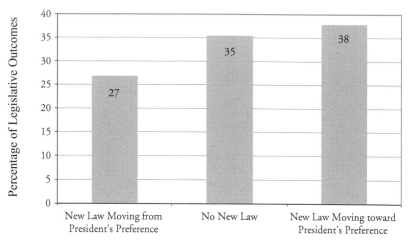

Figure 5.1 Legislative Outcomes Vis-à-Vis the President's Preference, 1953–2004.

Using data introduced in Chapter 4 and detailed in the Appendix, Figure 5.1 shows the distribution of legislative outcomes on major domestic policy issues vis-à-vis presidents' preferences. Since Eisenhower's inauguration, roughly two-thirds of the most important issues receiving serious congressional consideration have resulted in new laws.[1] And, despite the prevalence of divided government, most of those have been changes presidents supported rather than new laws they opposed.

Of course, the aggregate outcome pattern masks the considerable variation in different presidents' experiences. Figure 5.2 highlights this point, illustrating the distribution of legislative outcomes during each president's time in office. What we see is that while some presidents enjoyed frequent success on Capitol Hill, others found success more fleeting. For example, Presidents Johnson and Carter saw favorable outcomes on 78 percent and 62 percent of issues, respectively, which compares quite well to the 21 percent and 18 percent success rates experienced by Reagan and Ford. Moreover, while six of the ten most recent presidents have witnessed more laws moving toward their

---

[1] Because my research design focused on the most salient legislative debates (per coverage in *CQ Almanac*), this passage rate is almost surely higher than it would be in a random sample.

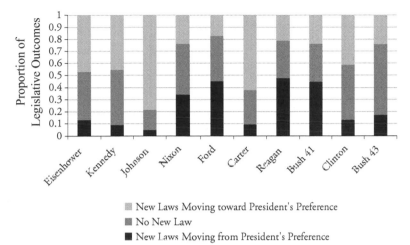

Figure 5.2 Legislative Outcomes Vis-à-Vis the President's Preference, by Administration. Excludes Congresses where the presidency switched hands – i.e., the Eighty-Eighth (Kennedy to Johnson) and Ninety-Third (Nixon to Ford). Also, data for President George W. Bush are limited to his first term.

preferred direction than away from it (Eisenhower, Kennedy, Johnson, Carter, Clinton, and Bush 43), four did not (Nixon, Ford, Reagan, and Bush 41).

An important, if somewhat obvious, point revealed in this analysis is that Democrats' partisan advantage in Congress through much of the postwar period was a boon to Democratic presidents and a bane to Republican ones. And, indeed, the greater pivotal voters' distance from each president's side, the worse the president fares on legislative outcomes. The bivariate correlation between new laws in the president's preferred direction and the president's distance from the House median voter is –.22, and that between new laws in the president's direction and his distance from the Senate filibuster pivot is –.25.

Interestingly, while other contextual variables also correlate with new laws moving as the president wishes, only an issue's salience and the president's political capital even approach the relationship seen with congressional variables. Table 5.1 details the bivariate correlations between laws moving in the president's preferred direction and relevant congressional, environmental, and issue-specific factors. Perhaps most unexpectedly, although presidential success is positively

TABLE 5.1. *Contextual correlates of a president's success,*
1953–2004

	Correlation with president's success
Congressional factors	
Divided government	−.30
House	
Senate	−.18
President to median: House	−.22
President to filibuster pivot: Senate	−.25
Environmental factors	
Honeymoon period	.10
Lame duck period	−.04
Tenure	−.03
President's political capital	.18
Positive exogenous events	.11
Negative exogenous events	.15
Issue factors	
Salience	.24
Civil rights	−.05
Community and housing	.04
Education	.04
Energy	−.01
Health	−.10
Social welfare	.03
Taxes	.12

Note: Dependent variable: indicates whether a new law moved in the president's preferred direction (1) or did not (0). The president's position and outcome were determined in a content analysis of each bill's corresponding *Congressional Quarterly Almanac* article. If the president had no role in an issue, we assumed that he preferred his standard predisposition (liberal for Democrats, conservative for Republicans). Among double-coded cases ($n = 249$), research assistants agreed on the outcome code in 97.6% and on presidents' position in 90.4%.

correlated with the honeymoon period and negatively correlated with the lame duck period, neither suggests a strong relationship. Furthermore, none of the issue areas provide especially fertile or treacherous policy turf, although health issues have been slightly less likely to produce presidential success, while tax issues have produced modestly more.

On balance, these preliminary results show that presidents' legislative success ebbs and flows primarily with the congressional tides. Presidents facing relatively close pivotal voters in both chambers have fared well overall (e.g., Lyndon Johnson), while those facing far-off pivotal voters have not (e.g., Gerald Ford). Beyond that, only ample political capital (a combination of high polling numbers and strong economic growth) and/or an especially newsworthy issue have appreciably correlated with presidential success after World War II.

That said, the question still unanswered, and the one I have emphasized throughout, is not whether presidents can overturn congressional predispositions across all issues and irrespective of Congress but rather whether they can systematically improve their chances on issues they actively engage and given whatever Congress they confront. Put differently, there is no doubting that presidents' legislative fortunes move in concert with congressional tides; still unclear, however, is whether presidents can propel forward in favorable currents or push through unfavorable ones. Chapter 4 showed that presidents' efforts do favorably affect the outcome of key roll-call votes. Now let me investigate White House officials' ability to move the nation's laws toward the president's preferred policy.

5.2 PUSHING LEGISLATION, PASSING LAWS

Obviously, presidents think that their lobbying campaigns can be effective. A central finding in the preceding chapter was that modern presidents have pushed for policies they support, regardless of the Congress or context they faced. For my purposes, this is important because it means that there is good reason to think that, all else being equal, any relationships of presidents' involvement and legislative success are causal. This begs the obvious follow-up question: Is presidents' involvement related to their success, or are presidents' legislative efforts largely symbolic gestures with little substantive impact?

5.2.1 Presidential Lobbying and Legislative Success

To begin interrogating presidents' impact on the overall outcome, Table 5.2 reports the overall pattern of each president's domestic legislative success by the level of his advocacy, 1953–2004. The first

TABLE 5.2. *New laws moving toward the president, by the president's involvement, 1953–2004*

	Of domestic initiatives considered, percentage resulting in new law moving toward president's position[a]			Diffference in win percentage, lobbied vs. no role
	Played no role	Endorsed a position	Actively lobbied	
Eisenhower	15%	50%	56%	+41
Kennedy	40%	21%	71%	+31
Johnson	63%	65%	89%	+26
Nixon	3%	29%	41%	+37
Ford	10%	13%	27%	+17
Carter	74%	64%	57%	−17
Reagan	3%	22%	39%	+36
Bush (41)	3%	40%	39%	+36
Clinton	13%	60%	59%	+46
Bush (43)	0%	10%	46%	+46
Mean (SD)	22% (26.8)	37% (21.1)	52% (18.0)	+30 (18.7)

Note: SD, standard deviation. Excludes Congresses where the presidency switched hands – i.e., the Eighty-Eighth (Kennedy to Johnson) and Ninety-Third (Nixon to Ford). Also, data for President George W. Bush are limited to his first term.

[a] On each issue, the president's position and outcome were determined through a content analysis of the corresponding *Congressional Quarterly Almanac* entry. If the president played no role in an issue, we assumed that he preferred his standard predisposition (liberal for Democrats, conservative for Republicans). Among double-coded cases ($n = 249$), research assistants agreed on the outcome code in 97.6% and on presidents' position in 90.4%. They agreed on the appropriate code for the president's involvement in 93.5% of double-coded cases.

finding is plain enough: presidents who have endorsed or lobbied on behalf of legislation have fared quite well. Only 22 percent of issues that presidents sat out ended in new laws moving toward their preferred position; this figure increases to 37 percent when the president advertised his position and 52 percent when the president actively lobbied on its behalf. At the broadest descriptive level, at least, presidents' involvement generally corresponded with greater success.

This bottom-line finding is somewhat misleading, however; beneath presidents' overall record of (clear but modest) success is considerable variation. While Lyndon Johnson and John F. Kennedy both enjoyed favorable outcomes on more than 70 percent of the domestic issues they lobbied for during their time in office, Gerald Ford and George W. Bush found success far harder to come by, even when they actively promoted their positions. Less than 40 percent of their lobbying campaigns ended with new laws moving in their preferred direction.

Then again, even as their overall levels of success have varied, it is important to realize that given the Congresses they faced, presidents' involvement has almost always been positively correlated with legislative success. This is true of presidents blessed with like-minded lawmakers (e.g., John Kennedy and Lyndon Johnson), cursed with disagreeable legislative lots (e.g., Gerald Ford and George H. W. Bush), or facing some combination of both (e.g., Dwight Eisenhower, Richard Nixon, Ronald Reagan, Bill Clinton, and George W. Bush).

The noteworthy exception is Jimmy Carter – the one president whose increased involvement corresponded with decreased success. Whereas 74 percent of the issues President Carter ignored ended up in national laws moving toward his preference, that success rate dropped to 64 percent for bills he endorsed, with another seven-point dip when he actually lobbied Congress.[2] So even though presidents' legislative involvement has generally correlated positively with success in Congress, important variations exist, including this one case where the White House's lobbying may have actually inhibited the president's success.

Beyond congressional predispositions, the other theoretically important extrapresidential variable affecting presidents' success is political capital. Like Congress' composition, political capital seems to affect the possible range of presidential success, but within those parameters, the White House's involvement contributes to whether the president's record pushes to the ceiling or settles on the floor. Figure 5.3 illustrates this by cutting the relationship between presidents' involvement and legislative success by their political capital. What we see is that presidents have indeed fared better when buoyed

---

[2] This is not the first time President Carter's efforts have appeared to be counterproductive. In one interesting study, Lee and Carol Sigelman (1981) demonstrated experimentally how attributing policies to President Carter *reduced* their public support. In the authors' words, Carter's support was thus akin to "the kiss of death" (1). In another, Mark Peterson (1990) also found President Carter's legislative record was markedly worse than would be expected given his context.

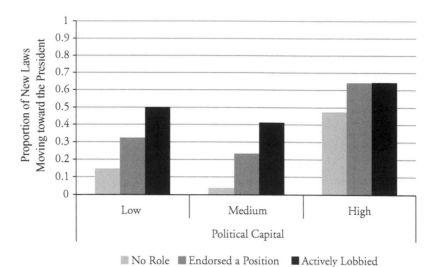

Figure 5.3 Presidential Involvement and Legislative Success, by Political Capital.

by a strong economy and high approval, with presidents signing preferred legislation twice as often in high-capital situations compared to low-capital ones. What is also obvious, though, is that given the particular political context, greater presidential involvement still corresponds with greater legislative success.

As before, these patterns support the claim that presidents' influence derives from both agenda setting and lobbying: for if it were the proposal per se (rather than the lobbying on its behalf) that principally determined presidents' success, greater effort would not generate greater success (as proposal powers are constant year-to-year, Congress-to-Congress, president-to-president). Furthermore, because presidents disproportionately target their "bully pulpit" at issues on which they oppose the status quo, if presidents' success reflected primarily agenda-setting powers, all presidents would enjoy high levels of success – largely irrespective of congressional composition or political context. So the fact that presidents' legislative success covaries with not only executive lobbying but also congressional composition and political context corroborates the notion that presidential success depends on more than issuing proposals. Lobbying is integral.

5.2.2 Presidential Lobbying and Legislative Success
on the Most Salient Issues

Of course, although presidents have not tailored their lobbying in response to pivotal voters' predispositions ($r = -.07$ for the House median, $-.04$ for the Senate pivot) or their own political capital ($r = .07$), presidents' involvement is correlated with an issue's salience ($r = .38$). This is hardly surprising, as presidents are attracted to salient issues and White House involvement only boosts their salience further. But it raises doubts about how much of the relationship between presidential lobbying and legislative success is actually rooted in the relationship between salience and success. Although I test this claim rigorously in the analyses that follow, it is useful to take a preliminary look here as well.

Table 5.3 lists the bivariate correlation between presidential lobbying and legislative success for all issues in the study, as well as for just the most salient ones (the top half). Comparing the two demonstrates that although particular coefficients vary somewhat, the overall relationship between presidential lobbying and new laws moving toward the president's position remains nearly identical ($r = .32$ overall and

TABLE 5.3. *Correlation of the president's involvement with legislative success, by salience*

	All issues	Most salient issues
Eisenhower	.29	.37
Kennedy	.34	.06
Johnson	.27	.47
Nixon	.38	.35
Ford	.18	−.17
Carter	−.15	−.29
Reagan	.40	.40
Bush (41)	.41	.44
Clinton	.42	.34
Bush (43)	.45	.43
Overall	.32	.29

Note: Excludes Congresses where the presidency switched hands – i.e., the Eighty-Eighth (Kennedy to Johnson) and Ninety-Third (Nixon to Ford). Also, data for President George W. Bush are limited to his first term.

$r = .29$ on the most salient issues).[3] Accordingly, these first-cut results indicate that even after mitigating differences in issue salience, presidents' lobbying is positively correlated with new laws moving in their preferred direction.

In short, the descriptive patterns are fairly clear: presidents' involvement in domestic lawmaking has typically corresponded with greater success, although not always. And while presidents' lobbying seems to be one important factor related to their success, numerous others also appear to be important – more important, in fact, than anything presidents do. The prospects for new laws moving in the president's preferred direction correlate, first, with congressional predispositions and, to a lesser degree, with the political context they occupy and the policy issues they tackle. The analytical task now becomes unpacking which of these relationships are substantively meaningful and which are merely a mirage.

5.3 TESTING PRESIDENTS' INFLUENCE ON LEGISLATIVE OUTCOMES, 1953–2004

The data presented to this point only indicate relevant factors' bivariate relationship with legislative outcomes that move the nation's laws toward the president's position. As such, there is good reason for concern that some of the relationships mentioned may be confounded by the others. There is also the important limitation that a simple correlation between two variables says nothing about the reliability (or lack thereof) of that baseline trend.

To help mitigate the complications associated with spuriousness and uncertainty, let me now utilize a multiple regression approach that accounts for the relevant relationships independent of the others while simultaneously specifying the statistical confidence associated with each. Using a theoretically derived specification does just this. It estimates presidents' impact on new laws independent of

---

[3] A minor but still noteworthy point is that the two presidents with the biggest difference in correlation coefficients for all issues versus just the most salient – i.e., Kennedy and Ford – are also the two for whom the data are based on the fewest cases. This is because both President Kennedy and President Ford served through just one full congressional term.

other factors and also accounts for the degree of uncertainty that estimate entails.

5.3.1   A Multiple (Probit) Regression Test

Revisiting the overarching theory, my argument has highlighted presidents' congressional fortune as turning on each chamber's pivotal voters and congressional leaders, as well as the president's political capital and his decisions about where to invest those persuasive assets. As the logic and variables correspond to those used in Chapter 4 (and detailed in the Appendix), I review them only briefly here. To capture pivotal voters' ideological predispositions, I include variables indicating the House median's and Senate filibuster pivot's ideological distance from the president's preferred side. Again, my theory, building from previous work, predicts that the closer the pivotal voters, the more likely the president's initiatives will ultimately become law.

To account for the different political winds that different presidents confront – at the back for some, in the face for others – the model includes a measure of presidential political capital. Using a factor score that merges the state of the economy with the president's approval ratings, I cut presidents' political clout in each Congress into thirds: low (1), medium (2), and high (3). My expectation is that presidents in high-capital situations will find lawmakers especially responsive to their appeals; presidents in low-capital situations will not.

The most important variable comes next: presidential involvement, which I have argued follows a combination of vote-centered and agenda-centered lobbying strategies. Drawing from each bill's legislative history in the relevant *Congressional Quarterly Almanac*, a research team coded presidents' involvement, including White House staffers and/or Cabinet officials, as none (beyond signing a new law) (0), endorsed a position (1), or actively lobbied (2). Research assistants agreed on the appropriate code for the president's involvement in 93.5 percent of double-coded cases ($n = 249$).

In addition to these theoretically important variables, the following analysis includes a myriad of control variables drawn from relevant political science research. Among these are several variables that control for distinctive periods in a president's term – that is, the honeymoon period, during the first half of his first term, and the lame duck

period, during the last half of his second term – as well as one captur-
ing his overall tenure. I also include a measure of exogenous events
in recognition that a range of other issues, from wars to scandals and
beyond, might distract the president, lawmakers, or both. Finally, the
model includes several issue-specific variables, such as each initiative's
salience and major policy domain (e.g., health, education, and taxes).

As the final point before turning to the analysis and results, it is
useful to recall that these data satisfy the empirical requirements I
have argued are necessary to test the theoretical hypotheses. First,
they capture the entire legislative process, earlygame to endgame,
and thus better account for the various places where presidents exert
influence. This is especially true because the model utilizes direct
measures of presidents' lobbying rather than indirect, omnibus measures of presidents' reputations. Also, and importantly, because the
dependent variable indicates each issue's ultimate outcome (rather
than a particular vote), it focuses attention exactly where presidents'
influence ought to be manifested: substantive changes to the nation's
laws. In short, the analyses that follow provide an especially valid test
of the theoretical model and its distinctive hypotheses. Accordingly,
let me now turn to the findings.

Table 5.4 reports the multiple regression results testing presidents'
influence on legislative outcomes controlling for the congressional,
environmental, and issue-specific factors that also determine whether
legislative debates end with new laws moving in the president's preferred direction. To examine how closely the empirical results dovetail
with theoretical predictions, I begin the discussion by looking at each
variable's impact holding all else constant at "typical" values.[4] For
comparison, the benchmark prediction in this "average" Congress
is that 39 percent of major domestic issues will be resolved by the
president signing into law legislation he supports (while 61 percent
will not).

---

[4] Estimates assume average pivotal voters, during a president's second Congress (non-
honeymoon, non-lame-duck), with the average number of exogenous events, when
the president wields medium political capital, and given a rather salient issue (+1
SD). To mitigate issue-specific variations, I hold the issue area at the average of all
issues. Finally, I assume that the president has endorsed a position but not lobbied
on its behalf.

TABLE 5.4. *Multiple regression of a president's legislative success, 1953–2004*

	Coefficient (robust SE)[a]	z-score
President to House median	−1.37 (.59)	−2.32**
President to Senate pivot	−1.24 (.55)	−2.26**
White House involvement	.28 (.07)	4.26**
Presidents' political capital	.46 (.07)	6.92**
Issue salience	.03 (.01)	2.54**
Key vote	−.28 (.16)	−1.79*
Honeymoon period	.22 (.16)	.1.37
Lame duck period	−.05 (.28)	−.19
President's tenure	.15 (.09)	1.63
Exogenous events	.10 (.03)	2.92**
Constant	.74 (.86)	.85
N	769	
log pseudolikelihood	−416.27	

Note: The model also allows fixed effects for each major issue (e.g., civil rights, education, and taxes). Dependent variable: bill resulting in a new law moving in the president's preferred direction (1) or not (0). The "not" category includes both bills that did not become law and bills that ended with a move the president opposed. *$p < .10$; **$p < .05$ (two-tailed).
[a] Standard errors (SE) are adjusted for clustering by each issue subtopic.

First, the president's policymaking outlook is significantly affected by pivotal voters' ideological predispositions. A greater policy distance between the president and congressional pivotal voters lowers the White House's chances for favorable outcomes. In the House, the baseline prediction of 39 percent success moves approximately six points for every standard deviation (SD) change in the House median's preference, from 27 percent with an especially disagreeable House pivot (+2 SD) to 52 percent with an especially sympathetic House swing voter (−2 SD). A similar finding emerges in the Senate, where comparable changes in the filibuster pivot's position increase the president's predicted success from 28 percent to 51 percent. And, not surprisingly, greater effects emerge if we change the two chambers' swing voters simultaneously – for example, when both House and Senate pivots change by ±2 SD. Here, the president's expected success rate varies by forty-six points, between 18 percent and 64 percent. Because the upper and lower chambers' pivotal voters tend to move together

($r = .64$), these results provide strong evidence that presidents' success is largely shaped by Congress' composition.

The second important variable class reflects the policymaking environment. Both the president's political capital and an issue's salience significantly delimit a president's legislative record. When prevailing political winds bolster the president's persuasiveness – that is, when the economy is strong and the president popular – his probability of penning preferred legislation jumps to one in two, compared to less than one-in-three odds when his political capital runs low. Additionally, the more salient an issue, the more likely it will pass, especially in the president's preferred direction. Pushing an issue from the fiftieth to the seventy-fifth salience percentile boosts the likelihood that it will end successfully for the White House by five points.[5]

Yet to say that nonpresidential factors affect presidents' potential success is not to say that presidents do not. If anything, the findings strongly affirm White House officials' legislative impact, even after controlling for the Congress and context they happen to inherit, as well as the salience of the issues they engage. A president who uses his considerable resources to advocate legislation significantly increases his prospects for ultimately signing a version of it into law. In an average Congress, with all else equal, his probability of success jumps from 23 percent if he plays no role to 57 percent if he chooses to lobby. I delve more deeply into this result later, but the bottom-line finding is unambiguous: although various contextual variables are statistically and substantively significant, accounting for presidents' lobbying remains centrally important to understanding their success.

The final insight from these results is what they say about key votes and presidential success. Returning to the theory (and Chap. 2), I argued that although both vote-centered and agenda-centered lobbying strategies can help presidents move laws in their preferred direction, the latter provide an especially profitable path to legislative success. In the context of this analysis, then, I hypothesized that

---

[5] The analysis further shows that among issue areas, civil rights and health are the two policy domains where presidents fare significantly worse, while taxes comprise the only area where presidents do significantly better. This was calculated using education as the referent category and holding all else equal.

a president's success is more likely when there is no key vote (all else being equal), which led me to add a variable indicating whether the bill had experienced a key vote (in either chamber).[6] The results corroborated this hypothesis. When a president lobbies for a bill in the average Congress characterized previously, the probability that his efforts will pay off with a signing ceremony is .48 if he must first win a key vote and .59 if he can find a way of circumventing such a floor fight. So even though this evidence is circumstantial and hardly conclusive, it nonetheless corroborates the argument that prosecuting the president's legislative agenda occasionally requires winning endgame floor fights but often does not.

5.3.2 Conditional Success

To better elucidate the implications of these findings for positive presidential power in Congress, I adopt the same approach I used in Chapter 4, illustrating the results' substantive significance by comparing predictions in two exemplar settings: the Eighty-Ninth (1965–66) and Ninety-Fourth (1975–76) Congresses. As a reminder, the first of these provided Lyndon Johnson an especially favorable combination of close pivotal voters and high political capital; the latter saddled Gerald Ford with a particularly unfavorable blend of distant pivotal voters and little political capital. Figure 5.4 shows the probability that a proposal will end up moving the nation's laws toward the president in these archetypes' settings (as well as in an average one).

Consistent with what we have seen throughout this book, theoretically and empirically, Congress and context again play a decisive role. Independent of the presidents themselves, the Eighty-Ninth Congress, in 1965, and the Ninety-Fourth Congress, in 1975, differed dramatically regarding the potential for president-supported success. In fact, a president who sat out an issue in the Eighty-Ninth Congress was still far more likely to see a new law move toward his preference than a

---

[6] Although the theoretical logic behind this test came well before any analysis, I should say that I did not originally include the "key vote" variable in the model but rather added it later when reflecting about how to disentangle earlygame and endgame lobbying in this section. Accordingly, these results reflect a more ad hoc examination and therefore demand further study.

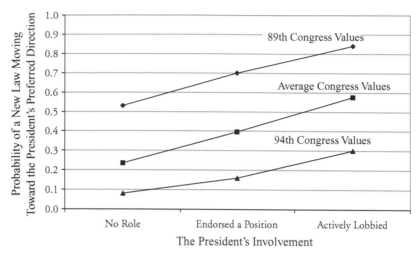

Figure 5.4 Predicted Probability of the President's Legislative Success.

president who actively lobbied for one in the Ninety-Fourth Congress. So, in the story of presidential leadership in lawmaking, a foremost consideration is the predispositions of potential (and pivotal) followers in Congress.

That being said, as important as congressional priors are, so too are presidents. In fact, given a particular setting and all else being equal, it is striking how much a president's lobbying can impact an issue's ultimate outcome. While the president's actively advocating a particular bill in a setting like the Ninety-Fourth Congress will yield preferred new laws less than one-third of the time, that is far better than the one-in-ten chances that prevail if he instead ignores the issue. Similarly, even in favorable settings, like that in the Eighty-Ninth Congress, a president's lobbying choices matter. A bill's odds for becoming law increase from one in two to seven in eight if it receives the White House's full-court press.

All told, then, president's legislative vehicles sail with the congressional currents, but not passively. When the president chooses to do so, he can help point proposals in his preferred direction and then help propel them to passage. Again, congressional and contextual factors delimit each president's legislative potential, but his involvement helps determine what, exactly, happens within that range.

5.3.3 Individual Differences?

To this point, presidents' *individual* effectiveness has played only a minor part in this study. The primary reason for this is theoretical: I believe that presidents' strategic choices and policy influence reflect institutional incentives rather than their personal traits. But a second, less high-minded reason has also played a part: the key-vote analysis simply did not include enough votes to provide reliable interpresident comparisons. By using data on overall outcomes, this chapter, in contrast, does include enough cases to afford a dependable look at each president.

Figure 5.5 presents the legislative success that each president actually experienced alongside the level predicted by the current model, 1953–2004. As a preliminary point, it is notable how well the parsimonious presidency-centered approach does predict each president's success (or lack thereof). The model accurately predicts the actual outcome in 72 percent of cases overall, including 78 percent of those issues where the prediction was more definitive (i.e., not between .4 and .6). And, as shown in the figure, the biggest discrepancies between actual and predicted success are for Lyndon Johnson (better than expected) and George W. Bush (worse than expected), but even there, the spreads between actual and predicted outcomes are modest.

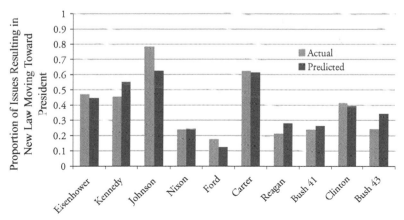

Figure 5.5 Actual and Predicted Levels of the President's Legislative Success. Excludes Congresses where the presidency switched hands – i.e., the Eighty-Eighth (Kennedy to Johnson) and Ninety-Third (Nixon to Ford). Also, data for President George W. Bush are limited to his first term.

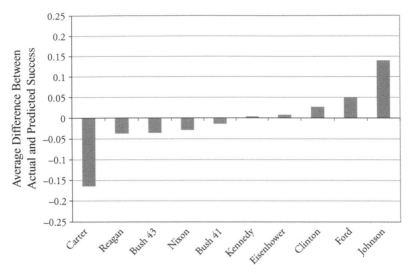

Figure 5.6 Difference between Actual and Predicted Success When Presidents Lobbied. Excludes Congresses where the presidency switched hands – i.e., the Eighty-Eighth (Kennedy to Johnson) and Ninety-Third (Nixon to Ford). Also, data for President George W. Bush are limited to his first term.

Yet even as the overall patterns seem to corroborate a presidency-centered approach that largely ignores each president's personal characteristics, one modestly countervailing piece of evidence deserves mention. In the earlier generation of research that extolled presidents' personal "skill," the core argument held that a president's personal impact is not seen on all issues but rather only when he uses it. To examine this claim more closely, Figure 5.6 shows the difference between the actual and the predicted success for issues *when the president lobbied.*

The results here are interesting. They show that although most presidents' success when lobbying was much as expected (within ±.05), two exceptions stand out: Lyndon Johnson did substantially better than the model predicts and Jimmy Carter did substantially worse. As I say, I have no particular explanation for this and, in fact, the differences are neither overwhelming nor even statistically significant.[7] However,

---

[7] I have argued that "skill" is properly conceptualized as the smart choice and effective execution of lobbying strategies, and that institutional resources (e.g., the

because they largely dovetail with the popular portrayals of presidents' "skill" – with President Johnson at the top, Carter at the bottom, and everyone else in between – they may leave open some avenues for studying presidential "skill" and legislative success.

5.4   CONCLUSION

For many of the day's most important, controversial public policy issues, it is the strategic interplay between the White House and Congress that determines the outcome. And, contrary to the popular critique that Washington is irrelevant to real people's lives, the truth is that legislative outcomes do have real-world consequences. On issues ranging from civil rights to public education, energy to health care, housing to taxes, what Congress passes or does not shapes the basic contours of American society.

Motivated precisely because the issues are so important, the stakes so high, all postwar presidents have leaped headlong into the lawmaking process – drafting preferred bills and pushing for their passage. The cornerstone of this project was my suspicion that these efforts are not executed in vain. And, indeed, the book's basic theory predicted that presidents' lobbying greatly boosts a proposal's chances of becoming law, even though that impact goes largely undetected in standard tests of presidential influence. Chapter 4, which found that a president's lobbying investments greatly improve his chances for reaching and winning key roll-call votes, bolstered this foremost hypothesis.

Still unexamined, however, was presidents' influence on the overall outcome. This is important because winning key votes and signing new laws, although certainly related, are not equivalent or even always consistently aligned. Rigorously testing White House aides' legislative impact thus required moving beyond key votes to appraisal of presidents' influence on legislative outcomes per se. This chapter has provided just such an appraisal.

To begin investigating presidents' impact on the bills that Congress passes (or does not), I first presented simple descriptive evidence

Office of Legislative Affairs) mute differences because all presidents get advice from Washington's best operators. In fact, one question relevant here is: How much of reputed skill is really a post hoc construction?

about the relationship between presidents' lobbying and legislative success. The results are telling. They show that for all but one president, greater legislative involvement has correlated positively with legislative success. On average, presidents who lobbied for a bill ended up signing supported new laws more than twice as often as presidents who played no active role. The glaring exception to this general rule is Jimmy Carter, the one chief executive who witnessed legislative success more often when he left the coalition building to Congress.

In light of the descriptive patterns hinting that presidents' persuasive efforts have often proved effective, I then turned to testing whether this inference was justified. Specifically, I tested whether presidents' influence held up even after accounting for a myriad of rival explanations, including congressional composition, political context, and issue specifics, as well as simple random chance. The results reveal a lot about the potential of presidential power and its limits.

First, as with the previous key-vote findings, this chapter reiterated that a president's ability to secure success is highly conditional. Indeed, presidents' prospects for passing preferred legislation depend greatly on the Congress and context in which they seek to do so. All else being equal, the more closely aligned pivotal voters' predispositions are with that of the president, the more he will find opportunities for achieving legislative success. Also of note are the contextual variables that delimit a president's potential success in Congress, including the president's political capital and the issue's salience. So, even within a Congress, these analyses show that presidents fare best when advocating salient issues and when backed by high approval ratings and a strong economy.

Still, presidents are not helpless prisoners of circumstance. Far from it. Even when facing decidedly unfavorable conditions – like those Gerald Ford inherited in 1974 – the president's decision to fight for legislation triples its odds of passing. So, although a 30 percent success rate may not inspire awe, it is far better than the 10 percent success rate the president would experience if not involved.

And a president's lobbying remains influential when his administration finds conditions more accommodating. Even with a Congress predisposed to support the president's agenda, his lobbying still greatly helps push his preferred initiatives to passage. Holding all else constant, when a president faces favorable circumstances, akin to those of Lyndon Johnson in 1965, his decision to advocate a bill boosts its chances of becoming law from a coin flip to a virtual lock.

Because the theory and findings summarized here had treated presidents as being equally effective (based on the idea that effectiveness is a function of the office, not the individual), section 5.3 examined this assumption's merits. The results show that accounting for presidents' involvement in an extrapresidential context largely explains their success. In fact, the model ignoring each president's particular characteristics accurately predicted legislative outcomes moving in their direction. However, there were two potential exceptions: Lyndon Johnson did somewhat better than expected and Jimmy Carter did somewhat worse. Because these two presidents are often said to embody the most and least skillful of legislative practitioners through the postwar period, this finding leaves open the possibility that individual presidents' "skill" may make a difference, albeit a relatively minor one.

Stepping back from the particulars, this chapter, as did the previous, has shown presidents to be powerful, but not all-powerful, players in federal policymaking. When the president decides that some particular policy initiative deserves his administration's backing, it is a great boon to the chances that a new law will supplant the old one. Yet also as predicted, this potential is constrained by Congress' pivotal voters, limited by the political environment, and variable by issue. Furthermore, although the president's involvement greatly increases the likelihood that a winning congressional coalition will be assembled, it is no guarantee. Indeed, the nature of presidential leadership in lawmaking is that, while it generally helps win key votes and pass preferred laws, it may not in any particular case.

CHAPTER SIX

The Practice and Potential of Presidential Leadership

The U.S. presidency occupies a special place in American politics. The office's extraordinary prestige is rivaled only by its distinguished pedigree. George Washington, Thomas Jefferson, Abraham Lincoln, and Franklin Roosevelt are more than predecessors; their monuments also reside mere blocks from the Oval Office. Is it any surprise that lofty expectations await those who serve in their shadow?

Unfortunately for today's occupants, the contemporary White House's legislative arsenal does not match its policy expectations. The Constitution simply does not provide the president any durable means for inducing legislators to consider his agenda, let alone pass it; and neither public opinion nor party ties can easily override that basic institutional setup. No wonder even the mild-mannered, generally successful President Eisenhower once snapped, "The selfishness of the members of Congress is incredible.... They are just about driving me nuts" (27 July 1954).

Considering the imposing obstacles presidents face when pushing legislation, one might wonder why today's chief executives continue making the effort. Are they just tap dancing before a demanding citizenry, or do presidents really think they can make a difference?

I have argued that presidents sincerely believe that their efforts matter, and I view this book's core contribution to be not just proving them right but also explaining why they are. The seminal discovery here is that presidential–congressional interactions in the earlygame are not ancillary to those in the endgame but rather provide a distinct and important decision-making venue. Building on this basic premise, I recast presidents' opportunities for influencing Congress and strategic options for best doing so.

While familiar tales of presidents' endgame plays for pivotal votes tell part of the story of president-led coalition building, they are far from the whole story. Indeed, they miss some of the most important parts. Instead of having to ply congressional centrists, I theorized (in Chap. 2) that administration officials can also build winning coalitions by pushing particular status quos onto the congressional calendar and then bargaining with leaders over which proposals surface as alternatives. So even though presidents sometimes find that their fate hinges on pivotal voters' preferences and the White House's ability to change them, other circumstances allow administration officials to circumvent pivotal voters rather than supplicate before them. The multifaceted empirical investigation corroborates the theory and its core predictions. The evidence shows that presidential lobbying tracts the strategies predicted (Chap. 3), and its impact is different (and greater) than previously realized, helping presidents win key votes (Chap. 4) and pass new laws (Chap. 5).

To avoid rehashing the arguments and evidence already discussed, however, I instead use this final chapter to consider the study's broader implications. Casting aside the all-too-familiar "great man" theories of presidential leadership, I offer a more modest take by highlighting the principled and pragmatic decisions that all presidents must make given the resources they control and the constraints they cannot. This does not yield any simple answers as to what "real" leadership entails, but it sets forth the trade-offs that real leaders must weigh. In doing so, this concluding chapter pulls the book's theoretical threads to help uncover the normative implications for citizens, scholars, and presidents alike.

6.1   THE PRACTICE OF PRESIDENTIAL LEADERSHIP

In the analysis of presidents' legislative leadership, one variable I cited as being unimportant stood out; unlike popular portraits of presidential power, my model eschews the notion that presidential leadership depends on each president's personal traits. Rather, I adopt

recent scholars' "presidency-centered" approach, based on the idea
that presidential–congressional relations are better explained by institutional opportunities and resources than individual will or skill.

Yet assuming that institutions are of paramount importance does
not mean that individual presidents are not. Far from it. My view is
that although the same basic factors shape each president's legislative
opportunities and lobbying resources, individual presidents' decisions
about how best to work within those parameters are vitally important.
Put differently, the presidency provides the levers of power, but it is up
to the president to decide which to pull. In this section, let me better
elucidate the important choices each president must make and their
implications.

6.1.1 Prioritizing Problems

Americans never see a shortage of national problems needing solutions. Reviewing Gallup's time-honored question about the "most
important problem facing the country today" reveals that postwar
Americans, in addition to frequently viewing the economy as prob-
lematic, have at various points also cited civil rights, energy, health
care, crime, and welfare as being among their most pressing concerns.
And, however much the omnibus categories paper over the particulars
(e.g., inflation versus unemployment versus taxes), they nonetheless
capture the essential point: salient, substantial problems always await
American presidents.

Before spelling out which problems are ripest for presidential picking, I should first note that presidents must pick; they must prioritize. On this score, President Jimmy Carter's experience is instructive.
Asked by a reporter if he would "be able to keep fully all [his] campaign promises," President Carter expressed his intention sincerely:
"My determination is to keep all those promises" (23 February 1977).
As became readily apparent, by insufficiently prioritizing certain initiatives, the Carter administration was unable to target resources effectively, from start to finish, earlygame to endgame. This basic error
helps explain why so much of President Carter's legislative agenda
languished on Capitol Hill.

Given that presidents must prioritize some problems, some initiatives, over others, an essential strategic question is deciding which

issue areas to elevate on the president's priority list. Which among the country's most important problems should the White House target for presidential involvement? Where should the president focus his policy attention and channel his legislative effort? A president's answer depends on both sincere and strategic considerations, and this book offers guidance regarding the latter.

Drawing on the logic underpinning this study, presidential advisors should target issues with an extreme status quo – that is, one far from the president's point of view and ideologically distant from what congressional "centrists" would prefer. Doing so virtually guarantees that the president can pass some policy closer to his preferred position because the president and Congress' swing voters agree not only that change is needed but also on the preferred direction for that change.

And the benefits of seeking to change a distant status quo do not stop there. Precisely because pivotal voters so dislike the current policy and are willing to support any number of alternatives to it, the president's *potential* for passing a policy closer to his ideal improves as well. Inasmuch as his vote-centered and agenda-centered lobbying prove effective, extreme status quos permit the president to make fundamental changes to the nation's laws rather than modest amendments.

Here again, perhaps the best way to demonstrate the importance of targeting distant status quos is to see what happens when a president does not. President George W. Bush's failed campaign to reform Social Security exemplifies this point. The essential difficulty miring the White House's offensive was not that the public strongly opposed the president's plan or that Democratic leaders outmaneuvered the administration. Instead, the fundamental problem plaguing President Bush's proposed reform was that "doing nothing" was always a viable option and, in fact, was a policy congressional moderates were always likely to support.[1] After all, the Congressional Budget Office projected that the status quo policy would pay full benefits for fifty years hence and cover approximately 80 percent of the promised benefits for years thereafter. So, regardless of President Bush's plan or strategy

---

[1] President Bush and his advisors recognized that the status quo, not the Democratic leaders' alternative, posed the greatest obstacle on the path to passage. To cast the status quo in the worst possible light, time and again the president argued that Social Security is "headed toward bankruptcy" and therefore needs to be "saved."

for selling it, the crux of the White House's strategic problem was that Congress' pivotal voters were already predisposed to support an easy, moderate alternative: making no changes whatsoever.

6.1.2   Drafting Policies

Picking the problems worth addressing is the first strategically important legislative decision presidents make; the second comes when a president's preferred solution is drafted. On this point, my model of presidential–congressional interactions uncovered some previously unrecognized lessons. Specifically, as important as fashioning a bill that appeals to Congress' pivotal voters may be, other considerations also demand attention: the White House should also look to "strengthen" leading allies' support and "soften" leading opponents' objections. The reason is that presidents' legislative prospects not only depend on sympathetic swing voters but also can improve greatly inasmuch as a president's leading allies advocate his policy (rather than their own) and leading opponents decide to cut a deal early rather than fight till the end.

One way to satisfy these strategic aims – that is, attracting swing voters, rallying leading allies, and deterring leading opponents – is simply to identify "wedge" issues that consolidate supporters and divide opponents. Identifying such issues depends on the particular constellation of congressional leaders and swing voters, not to mention the nation's problems and president's preferences. However, recent history has shown tax cuts to be a good wedge issue for Republican presidents, while Democratic presidents have similarly benefited on education issues.

When the policy area itself does not satisfy the White House's proximate political objectives – that is, rallying leading allies, deterring leading opponents, and attracting swing voters – then the president and his team must be more creative. In particular, the administration should consider including various "sweeteners" that leading allies, leading opponents, or pivotal voters value intensely.[2] As

---

[2]   Similarly, if leading allies, leading opponents, or swing voters find a particular provision especially objectionable, the White House should consider modifying it, if not omitting it. This does not mean that the president should grant these strategically

before, the exact elements potentially included depend on the particular lawmakers involved. For example, if an opposing leader generally opposes a president's education plan but, for whatever reason, cares deeply about special-education funding, the administration should consider adding extra special-education funding to its bill *if doing so will offset the opposing leader's objections to the president's preferred provisions.*

This leads to yet another important point about White House bill drafting: presidential aides should know what the president ideally wants but not anchor him to that position; they must leave "wiggle room." Again, deal making is essential to presidential leadership, so rather than publicly commit the president to a detailed legislative program, much less propose one, White House staffers should instead draw some clear lines regarding the president's preferred provisions while simultaneously leaving room for adjustments as negotiations proceed and deals are struck.[3]

Perhaps the most illuminating bill-drafting case is seen in the Clinton administration's attempt at health-care reform. There, Hillary Clinton fashioned the administration's (1,300-page) proposal with administration allies alone, largely indifferent to strategic congressional consideration. The result was a spectacular failure. Mere days after making the task force's recommendations public, Senate Finance Committee Chairman Daniel Patrick Moynihan (D-NY) declared, "Anyone who thinks [the Clinton health care plan] can work in the real world as presently written isn't living in it." *Time* reporters, in light of this and comparable statements, saw the writing on the wall: "Slowly but surely, Bill Clinton's health-care plan is headed for the triage unit" (31 January 1994).

In short, because presidential initiatives so often serve as the starting point for legislative debates, Washington insiders care deeply about the contents of presidential pronouncements. The proposal-drafting

---

positioned members veto power over his bills, just that it may often be in the president's strategic interest to consider cutting provisions that certain members' deem "deal breakers."

3   President Clinton and his team subsequently took to proposing general "principles" rather than detailed bills. President George W. Bush adopted the latter approach throughout his term, and early reports show that President Obama has as well.

process thus affords presidents an important strategic opportunity. By folding into the president's plan provisions that strengthen leading allies, soften leading opponents, and/or attract pivotal voters, an administration can help "grease the skids," as they say in the capitol, and set the stage for the lobbying campaign that will follow.

6.1.3   Devising Strategy

I have written extensively about the vote-centered and agenda-centered lobbying strategies that presidents have available. I have also offered an in-depth look at the conditions under which each, or some combination of both, should prove effective (a function of the status quo; supportive and opposing leaders' preferences, along with that of the pivotal voter; and the president's political capital). With an issue and initiative in hand, the theory exposed White House advisors' assignment to be identifying their particular conditions and applying the optimal strategic blend.

Here is where the distance between theory and practice is greatest. The stylized theory presumes that each context can be known precisely and, in fact, that presidents and lawmakers know it. Reality is far murkier. Where, exactly, is the status quo located? How much political capital does the president wield? What is an opposing leader's preference on the issue, and what will induce him or her to alter that position? What do pivotal voters' want now, and where are they likely to end up?

In answering these questions, the first problem presidential advisors face is pervasive uncertainty. This estimation challenge has a myriad of causes, not the least of which is the ever-changing "real world," in which congressional members have countervailing incentives. Adding to lawmakers' sincere preference uncertainty is a penchant for strategic ambiguity, if not purposeful dissembling. The implications inside the West Wing are profound: estimating one legislator's position is hard in any case, and it is harder still when attempting to do so at some undetermined future point.

In addition, because all lawmakers (but especially congressional leaders) tailor their actions based on what they expect their colleagues to do, forecasting the policy wishes of one lawmaker at a time is not enough. After all, arm-twisting one member and/or cutting a deal with another will affect not just that member's choices but also his or her colleagues'. Unintended consequences can greatly complicate the administration's strategic game plan. So rather than analyze each member in isolation, presidents and their aides must also consider the interrelationships among Congress' 535 members, within and between parties, across two chambers. We can now see why the seemingly uncomplicated task of discerning the White House's optimal lobbying strategy is anything but.

A final point about the White House's congressional game plan deserves mention. In Chapter 3, I distinguished lobbying strategies from lobbying tactics: I defined lobbying *strategies* as the general prescriptions a White House uses to promote presidential policies in all contexts. By contrast, I defined lobbying *tactics* as the specific techniques, practices, and methods employed to carry out a lobbying strategy in a particular instance. As stated before, this book explains the general strategies presidents may execute in any case, not the particular tactics best suited to a particular case.

In many ways, then, Legislative Affairs advisors' expertise kicks in where my theory leaves off. For these executive office insiders, calculating strategic options is more or less second nature; the more challenging decision making comes in figuring out the optimal tactics that follow. Presidential aides often have an "intuitive" feel that it is better to cut a deal with a leading opponent than to try to beat him or her on the floor; but, even so, the president's Legislative Affairs team requires extensive analysis to determine how best to approach that opposing leader. In practice, such tactical-level deliberations are commonplace.[4] So, although it is beyond the scope of this project, tactical decision making remains centrally important for practitioners devising the White House's legislative strategy. Actually, it is one of the areas where their discretion is the greatest and a particular president's "skill" might actually make a modest difference.

---

4 In one case, a key Clinton administration official explained to me how the Legislative Affairs team often contemplated who should call different lawmakers, President Clinton or Vice President Gore. As he told it, "The President was the good cop; the Vice President was the bad cop. President Clinton would listen carefully to what they had to say. . . . Vice President Gore would, well, let me put it this way, we called him the 'nut-cutter.'"

6.1.4 Executing

Having prioritized a problem, drafted a preferred policy, devised a lobbying strategy, and planned its tactical implementation, the White House's last area for legislative discretion comes into focus: execution. Although seemingly a mere task of translation, implementing the administration's lobbying strategy actually requires a Herculean effort. Nick Calio, chief lobbyist for both President Bushes (41 and 43), captured the assignment well: "The most important thing was we were on Capitol Hill all the time – I mean, all the time. We became familiar sights; people on both sides of the aisle were very comfortable with seeing us; they expected to see us. They consequently would talk to us, all the time" (Patterson 2000, 116).

Interestingly, several elements endemic to this congressional liaison work can undermine a president's effectiveness in advocating his agenda. For one thing, the extensive nature of interactions between Legislative Affairs officials and members of Congress can have a drawback: White House staffers explicitly charged with "congressional relations" may prioritize "good relations" ahead of "good policy." This cross pressure explains why the administration's "policy people" sometimes worry that Legislative Affairs aides are too sympathetic to congressional wishes – recommending the path of least resistance rather than the path of maximal influence. For a president looking to influence lawmakers and legislation, the corresponding challenge is making sure that presidential–congressional relations are a means to policy ends, not an end unto itself.

The second obstacle to executing the administration's lobbying campaign arises because Congress offers so many diversions. In addition to promoting presidential initiatives, Legislative Affairs staffers are responsible for tending to members' queries, monitoring other legislative issues, and advising executive nominees or witnesses headed to Capitol Hill. The problem for presidents is that the latter tasks, however important, can compromise the first: executing the initial strategic plan and then updating it in light of new information or changing circumstances. So, here again, a precursor to executing the president's lobbying campaign effectively is first to maintain the White House staff's focus and discipline.

The final, familiar hurdle to effective lobbying is that "the administration" is not a singular entity but rather a diverse hodgepodge of offices and officials. This heterogeneity, as any Chief of Staff knows well, spawns one of the White House's foremost dilemmas: the president's agenda is not necessarily the agenda of everyone in his administration. Obviously, when administration officials (augmented by their own office's legislative affairs outfit) work at cross-purposes, they greatly undercut the president's case. Part of executing a lobbying strategy, therefore, is suppressing internal dissent and ensuring intra-administration coordination.[5] President Clinton's Assistant to the President for Legislative Affairs, Patrick Griffin, emphasized the point: "I did not want anybody up there who was off-message.... If people were getting away from us, they would be snapped back into line – on the big issues" (Patterson 2000, 127).

In short, contrasted against the theoretical purity of planning a lobbying campaign, the practice of executing that campaign often appears untidy. In addition to the omnipresent distractions, those pushing the president's preferred bill find that others often push back. Such challenges render executing the administration's legislative strategy as important as devising it. On the ground, the distinction between strategizing and executing fades as the process unfolds; doing either one well requires doing both well.

6.2 PRINCIPLE VERSUS PRAGMATISM

In the preceding discussion, as in the theory before, I assume a pragmatic president. That is, I have envisioned presidents as being motivated by policy goals and agitating to push for them but willing to accept concessions that facilitate passage. Thus, my theory's presidents exemplify the old saw, "Don't make the perfect the enemy of the good."

Pragmatism's strategic significance is certainly an important point, one that modern presidents have typically heeded, especially when

---

[5] Difficulties in getting administration officials "onboard" with the president's agenda are so endemic to the presidency that one presidential aide told Thomas Cronin (1970), "Everybody believes in democracy until he gets to the White House."

facing an oppositional Congress. The examples are now familiar: Eisenhower on civil rights; Nixon on revenue sharing, Clinton on welfare, Bush (41) on the budget. Even Ronald Reagan, contrary to popular remembrances, happily endorsed substantive compromises that helped get his bills through the capitol. Biographer Lou Cannon (2000) explained President Reagan's perspective: "Conservative sniping from outside the White House at the 'pragmatism' of [his advisors] had little impact on the president because Reagan at the time shared the political realism of his aides. . . . He often complained that some of his erstwhile conservative supports wanted to go 'off the cliff with all flags flying'" (90).

But not all presidents have been eager to belly up to the negotiating table. Here, Jimmy Carter's disdain for legislative give-and-take stands out. Time and again, President Carter was loathe to endorse anything short of his sincere preferences. With provisions of his National Energy Plan still being hammered out on Capitol Hill, a reporter asked the president about the negotiations, particularly his take on concessions sought by Senator Russell Long (D-LA), Finance Committee Chairman. President Carter's response was typical of his instinct to prioritize principle over pragmatism:

> We will add our assistance when we can, but we will not betray the confidence of people who look to us for leadership. And I will not work out any private agreement with Senator Long that would betray the commitments that we've made previously, publicly, I might say, in all instances. So, I don't see any possibility of doing what you propose, or what you ask about. (30 November 1977)

However gratifying sticking to principle may seem intuitively, such intransigence is ultimately counterproductive. If the president's goal is getting principled beliefs implemented as national policy, he must negotiate, compromise, and occasionally concede. In other words, policy-motivated presidents must bargain.

On the other hand, it is important to recall that congressional passage of a bill is sometimes a president's secondary consideration. These are times when the president perceives a greater good than legislative change, thereby leading him to privilege rhetorical purity and/or moral clarity over signing of new legislation. Put differently, there are situations in which presidents value presidential leadership *outside* lawmaking over presidential leadership *in* lawmaking. Obviously, this is a perfectly legitimate decision, sometimes even an admirable one. And, either way, that presidents' choice between principle and pragmatism implicates their legislative effectiveness only affirms that individual presidents' particular choices can matter.

6.3   BIGGER THAN WINNING

This book has followed a long, distinguished tradition of examining presidential power on legislative outcomes. The primary reason, of course, is that outcomes have consequences, laws have consequences. And, as Richard Neustadt (1990[1960]) eloquently proclaimed, "[A president's] impact on the outcome is the measure of the man. His strength or weakness, then, turns on his personal capacity to influence the conduct of the men who make up government. His influence becomes the mark of leadership" (4).

In the main, I subscribe to Neustadt's standard. After all, a basic premise behind this book generally, and this conclusion specifically, is that public policy provides the basic motivation for presidents to lobby and offers the fundamental standard of their success. Occasions for influencing congressional lawmaking always arise, so integral to appraising any president's legacy is examining how effectively he recognizes and capitalizes on his office's potential.

Yet as important as policy outcomes may be, they are not all that is important. The process itself is as well. In a republic like ours, there is intrinsic value in debating important, controversial issues, and more still in making lawmakers articulate clear positions on those issues. Indeed, the democratic virtues of robust policy debate in Congress hold true independent of who or what prevails.

On the matter of process qua process, the simple fact of the matter is that contemporary presidents have unmatched potential for animating America's policymaking apparatus. Presidents spur public debate and, just as important, legislative debate. And, precisely because presidents' advocacy provides the political engine for so many policy debates, it is noteworthy that presidential lobbying's significance extends beyond its impact on congressional outcomes and to congressional process. It is a point that Teddy Roosevelt famously (and forcefully) noted:

> It is not the critic who counts; not the man who points out how the strong man stumbles, or where the doer of deeds could have done them better. The credit belongs to the man who is actually in the arena, whose face is marred by dust and sweat and blood; who strives valiantly; who errs, who comes short again and again, because there is no effort without error and shortcoming; but who does actually strive to do the deeds; who knows great enthusiasms, the great devotions; who spends himself in a worthy cause; who at the best knows in the end the triumph of high achievement, and who at the worst, if he fails, at least fails while daring greatly, so that his place shall never be with those cold and timid souls who neither know victory nor defeat. (23 April 1910)

As the final point, then, it is worth recalling that a prerequisite to winning legislative debates is getting into them. So even if presidents are graded largely on the curve of outcomes, all deserve some credit for putting themselves into the policymaking game, for seeking potential successes and accepting the possibility of failure. This is as true for President Johnson, for whom legislative success was likely, as it is for President Ford, for whom winning was always a long shot. In this sense, I fully subscribe to President Eisenhower's observation: "I'll tell you what leadership is: it's persuasion, and conciliation, and education, and patience. It's long, slow, tough work" (Hughes 1963, 124).

Archival Study Technical Details

Lyndon Johnson counseled presidents to shepherd initiatives "from cradle to grave," adding, "There is but one way for a president to deal with Congress, and that is continuously, incessantly, and without interruption. If it is really going to work, the relationship has got to be almost incestuous" (Kearns Goodwin 1991, 226). The abstract theory that comprises this book's analytic core has put social science meat on Lyndon Johnson's intuitive bone. Specifically, I have theorized that before lobbying pivotal voters in the legislative endgame, presidents can also lobby congressional leaders in the legislative earlygame.

Given the paths by which presidents may seek influence in Congress, the follow-up question is obvious: Do they work? That is, can a presidents' lobbying affect the outcome of "key" roll-call votes, the content of the nation's laws? The answers to these questions are the subjects of Chapters 4 and 5. Here, I report the technical details of the study that yielded those data.

A.1 RESEARCH DESIGN

Part and parcel of my argument about presidential coalition building is that properly appraising it requires accounting for the entire legislative process – "from cradle to grave," as President Johnson put it. In testing presidents' influence, therefore, the archival study described here sought to gather valid data that account for both voting and prevoting processes. I further sought data that included a myriad of contexts, spanning different presidents and Congresses, and that emphasized major domestic policy debates during the postwar period.

To these ends, the first task in this study was setting its basic parameters. There, thankfully, I was able to draw on the Policy Agendas Project (www.policyagendas.org) and its coding of each *Congressional Quarterly (CQ) Almanac* for seven major domestic policy domains – civil rights, community and housing, education, energy, health, social welfare, and taxes – and the fifty-five corresponding subtopics.[1] These topics, listed in Table A.1, were selected for study because they have comprised the most important venues for settling ideological debates about the nation's social and economic policy. Empirically, they comprise the population of domestic policy domains that could be addressed in each Congress.

With the issue areas identified, the next task was identifying whether a relevant bill had received "serious consideration" in each Congress (see also Edwards, Barrett, and Peake 1997; Edwards and Barrett 2000). Fortunately, here again, the Policy Agendas Project helped uncover the answer. The project used *CQ Almanac*'s annual review of legislative initiatives to identify and organize each Congress from the 83rd (1953–54) to the 107th (2001–2) (inclusive) by issue area. When multiple initiatives were considered in a particular issue area, the one included in the study is the one that received the greatest amount of coverage, which I took to be an indication of the issue's newsworthiness – its importance, controversy, and involvement of key players. I did this with the idea that these are the ones most likely to attract presidential involvement, whether or not they did in any particular instance. Also, if an initiative was described in each of the two years of a Congress, the latter of the two was coded, ensuring the most up-to-date coding. Finally, using the same issue areas, I updated the data through the 108th Congress. The upshot: the sampling frame included 1,430 potential domestic issue areas from 1953 to 2004, which ultimately yielded 769 congressional initiatives that received serious consideration.

---

[1]   The decision to focus on domestic policies was based on the likely possibility that presidential–congressional interactions in matters of foreign policy are different in important ways (see Canes-Wrone, Howell, and Lewis 2008; Wildavsky 1969).

TABLE A.1. *The sample frame for domestic policy issues*

Major policy category/specific issue area (Policy Agenda code)

Civil rights (2)

General (200)
Age discrimination (204)
Ethnic/racial discrimination (201)
Gender/sex discrimination (202)
Handicap or disease discrimination (205)
Voting rights (206)

Community development and housing (14)

General (1400)
Elderly and handicapped housing (1408)
Housing and community (1401)
Housing for the homeless (1409)
Low/middle-income housing (1406)
Rural economic (1405)
Rural housing (1404)
Secondary mortgage market (1410)
Urban economic development (1403)
Veterans housing (1408)

Education (6)

General (600)
Arts and humanities (609)
Education of underprivileged (603)
Educational excellence (607)
Elementary and secondary (602)
Higher education (601)
Special education (606)
Vocational (604)

Energy (8)

General (800)
Alternative and renewable (806)
Coal (805)
Electric and hydroelectricity (802)
Energy conservation (807)
Natural gas and oil (803)
Nuclear (801)

(continued)

TABLE A.1. *(continued)*

Major policy category specific issue area (Policy Agenda code)

Health (3)

General (300)
Alcohol (342)
Comprehensive health reform (301)
Controlled and illegal (343)
Facilitates, construction (322)
Health manpower and training
Infants and children (332)
Insurance reform (302)
Long-term care (334)
Medical liability (324)
Mental health (333)
Prescription drug (335)
Prevention, communicable diseases (331)
Regulation of drugs, etc. (321)
Research and development (398)
Tobacco (341)

Social welfare (13)

General (1300)
Assistance to the disabled (1304)
Elderly issues (1303)
Food stamps (1301)
Poverty (1302)
Social services and volunteer (1305)

Macroeconomics (1)

Tax policy and tax reform (107)

Source: Policy Agendas Project (www.policyagendas.org).

Figure A.1 displays the sample's policy-domain distribution. The greatest proportion of initiatives addresses health (27 percent), followed by comparable numbers of bills regarding education (17 percent), community and housing (16 percent), energy (15 percent), social welfare (13 percent), and civil rights (9 percent). Tax bills comprise the smallest portion of the sample (3 percent). The distribution is quite similar among the most salient half of the bills, although health drops to 21 percent of the sample, while tax initiatives increase to 6 percent.

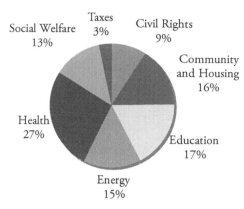

Figure A.1 The Sample's Distribution of Policy Domains.

Having selected the bills for the study, the next task was to capture the essential details about each. Let me now explain these measures, starting with the dependent variables (winning key votes, discussed in Chap. 4, and passing preferred laws, in Chap. 5) and proceeding to the independent and control variables.

A.1.1 Dependent Variables

As noted elsewhere, the foremost empirical challenge in appraising presidential influence is the lack of a precise measure of policy content; there is no standard to judge one policy as "n units" more liberal or conservative than another. Absent a fine-grained measure of policies' substance, researchers have instead had to rely on indirect measures of policy outcomes and, in turn, presidential influence. Of course, the better the indirect measures, the better the inferences they afford. Here, I sought two dependent variables – one about voting, one about the overall outcome – that offered especially valid indicators of congressional outcomes.

A.1.1.1 Winning key votes. The two most common approaches to measuring presidents' record on roll-call votes are exemplified by George Edwards (1989), on the one hand, and Jon Bond and Richard Fleisher (1990), on the other. In Edwards' study, he analyzed members' average annual support for the president's position across different classes of votes,[2] which allowed him to unpack the congressional coalitions that support and oppose presidents. Bond and Fleisher (1990) focused on a related but distinct question and, accordingly, employed a different measure. Rather than look at who supported/opposed the president's position, the authors instead examined whether the president's side prevailed (see also Fleisher and Bond 2000). The latter measure is equivalent to Cox and McCubbins' (2005) concept and measure of a "roll" but applied to presidents rather than lawmakers. Accordingly, a president is "rolled" when he sides against the winning coalition; he "wins" when his position ultimately prevails.

For my purposes, Bond and Fleisher's (and Cox and McCubbins') measure is most appropriate; the binary win–lose measure best corresponds to my substantive focus: presidents' influence over policy outcomes. Although not ideal – as noted, an interval-level content measure would be preferable – winning crucial votes is nonetheless an integral part of affecting outcomes. Knowing whether the president's side ultimately prevailed thus allows me to investigate the systematic factors contributing to that success/failure, including presidents' role therein or lack thereof. Also desirable, this measure provides an absolute standard of success, thereby allowing equivalent comparisons across presidents, Congresses, issues, and the like.

Its virtues noted, some caveats about this dependent variable's validity demand attention. As many have noted (see Arnold 1990; Bond and Fleisher 1990, chap. 3; Edwards 1989, chap. 2; Jones 1994, 192–195; M. Peterson 1990, app. B; Rudalevige 2002, chap. 7), roll-call–based measures like the one I employ permit valid inferences only inasmuch as we accurately map the vote to the policy outcome and also inasmuch as presidents do not strategically tailor their positions (or their public declarations) to inflate their successes and/or mask their failures. When these two conditions are satisfied, roll-call votes validly tap the construct of interest: presidents' success or failure on a given issue.

---

[2] The votes analyzed included all those where presidents stated their preferred outcome, as well as subsets therein, including only contested votes (at least 20% opposing the majority) or those flagged as "key" by CQ staff (see Bond and Fleisher 1990, 60; Edwards 1989, chap. 2).

To meet the first demand – that the vote accurately reflects the relevant outcome – the analysis that follows uses only *CQ*'s tally of "key" votes – votes explicitly chosen because they indicate "a matter of major controversy, a test of presidential or political power, and a decision of potentially great impact on the nation and on lives of Americans" (*CQ Weekly*, 1 January 2007, 60; see also Bond and Fleisher 1990; Edwards 1989; Shull and Vanderleeuw 1987). To meet the second requirement – that presidents do not engage in strategic position taking – I include not just votes where presidents publicly announced their position, but also votes where they did not. To do so, I assume that when presidents did not announce a preference, their position is consistent with that of their party's median member.

All told, then, for each initiative in the sample, research assistants coded, first, whether it included a *CQ* key vote and, second, whether the president's side won or lost. Again, to mitigate presidents' strategic dissembling or position taking, I assumed that when the president did not explicitly announce his preferred position, his preference matched that of his party's chamber median. The same process was repeated for both the Senate and the House. The result of this was that of the 769 initiatives identified, 100 were subject to a Senate key vote and 113 to a House key vote.

Comparing presidents' success in the total population of domestic key votes versus those in my sample reveals the similarities. As shown in Figure A.2, the president won 62 percent of key House votes overall and 69 percent of those in the sample; in the Senate, presidents won 61 percent and 62 percent among all and sampled domestic votes, respectively. So while presidents fare slightly better on the sampled key votes than on all key votes in both chambers, the difference is not statistically significant in either chamber.

Table A.2 drills even deeper into the overall-versus-sample differences, reporting the respective success rates for each president. The results again suggest that the sample largely reflects the population, although some differences can be seen. Such divergences, however, are generally found for the presidents with the fewest sampled key votes. For example, the biggest discrepancy between the sample and the population of domestic key votes is seen in President Ford's Senate record, but that is because President Ford only has three key Senate

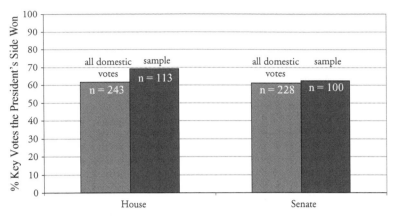

Figure A.2 President's Success in *Congressional Quarterly*'s Key Votes, by President, 1953–2004. Domestic policy key votes are defined as those primarily about civil rights, community and housing, education, energy, health, social welfare, or taxes.

TABLE A.2. *President's success in* Congressional Quarterly's *key votes, by president, 1953–2004*

President's percentage of wins on key votes (total no. of key votes)					
House of Representatives			U.S. Senate		
All domestic key votes	Sample key votes	President	All domestic key votes	Sample key votes	
83% (18)	83% (12)	Eisenhower	65% (20)	40% (10)	
50% (8)	50% (4)	Kennedy	82% (11)	67% (6)	
85% (27)	86% (14)	Johnson	83% (29)	91% (11)	
74% (35)	79% (14)	Nixon	55% (31)	60% (10)	
58% (19)	67% (3)	Ford	36% (14)	0 (3)	
50% (26)	40% (10)	Carter	61% (23)	64% (11)	
52% (33)	63% (16)	Reagan	79% (28)	88% (8)	
38% (21)	43% (7)	Bush (41)	48% (21)	50% (8)	
53% (38)	67% (12)	Clinton	55% (31)	50% (10)	
72% (18)	75% (12)	Bush (43)	40% (20)	55% (11)	
H_{null}: $\mu_{all} - \mu_{sample} = 0$			H_{null}: $\mu_{all} - \mu_{sample} = 0$		
$p = .41$			$p = .86$		

Note: The table excludes Congresses where the presidency switched hands – i.e., the Eighty-Eighth (Kennedy to Johnson) and Ninety-Third (Nixon to Ford). Also, data for President George W. Bush are limited to his first term.

votes in the sample. Accordingly, an important lesson going forward is that inferences based on all presidents' key vote records are credible; inferences about each president's particular results are not.

A.1.1.2 Passing preferred laws. As integral as roll-call votes are to determining legislative outcomes, the two are not synonymous. Citing the distinction, several researchers have executed studies using alternate, nonvoting-based measures of policy outcomes. Mark Peterson (1990) looked at presidents' proposals and coded outcomes in terms of whose preference (the president's or Congress' or neither) "dominated," while Rudalevidge (2002) (with presidential proposals) and Barrett and Eshbaugh-Soha (2007) (with significant new laws) coded the overall outcome in Congress vis-à-vis the president's stated position, from getting "virtually everything" he wanted to getting "nothing like what he wanted." Such approaches have proven instructive, partly because these operationalizations are more closely aligned with the theoretical construct: policy outcomes.

At the same time, however, these nonvoting measures suffer in that their standards are not absolute across all presidents, Congresses, and policies. For example, two presidents with identical preferences and equivalent legislative outcomes could receive a significantly different score if one proposed his ideal and the other moderated his proposal to satisfy public opinion, not to mention congressional realities (with the former appearing to fare far worse than the latter).

In light of these considerations, I sought a non-roll-call–based dependent variable that met two requirements. First, it should assess the overall change in policy (rather than any particular decision), and second, it should be based on absolute standards of success (rather than depending on presidents'/congressional leaders' revealed preferences). If we can develop such a measure, we can get not only a valid assessment of the outcome but also one that is comparable for all presidents, in all Congresses, for all issues.

A variable that meets these criteria is one indicating whether a new law passed and, if so, in which ideological direction the law shifted – toward the president's position or away from it. To create such a measure, for each initiative receiving serious consideration in our sample (already discussed), we first coded the outcome as one of four categories: no new law (stuck in Congress), no new law (presidential veto sustained), new law (passed and signed), new law (veto overridden). The intercoder reliability showed that the research assistants identified the same outcome code more than 97 percent of the time.[3] The second portion of the measure asked for the president's assessment of the outcome, with codes of "likes a lot," "mostly likes," "mostly dislikes," "dislikes a lot," and "administration not mentioned."[4] The two "likes" categories were merged into one code and the two "dislikes" into another (94 percent coder agreement). Combining these two variables gave us a measure indicating whether a new law passed and, if so, whether it was in the president's preferred direction. Finally, to deal with bills on which the president had not publicly stated a position, we assumed that his position was his typical one.[5] Thus, we also coded "who was happier with the final outcome: liberal Democrats or conservative Republicans" (93 percent coder agreement). In sum, the dependent variable here indicated whether each issue ended by moving the nation's laws toward the president's position (1) or not (0).

A.1.1.3 Accounting for the earlygame and endgame.

One more important point about these dependent variables deserves emphasis: both allow me to account for the entire legislative process, from the earlygame to the endgame. Specifically, I am able to include all 769 bills that received congressional consideration in the analyses, not just the ones that made it to the floor, much less to a key vote.[6] With the passing-preferred-laws variable, this is easy because all bills either

---

[3] On this measure, as on all others, when the two research assistants diverged, I went back and redid the coding. My final code is the one included in the dataset.

[4] To identify the president's position, we considered his statements and activities taken as a whole. For example, a president who repeatedly spoke out against a bill but supported it just before final passage or when signing it into law was still coded as "dislikes" the outcome if its contents had not changed.

[5] This struck us as a reasonable decision considering that 89% of presidents' announced positions matched their standard predisposition – liberal for Democrats, conservative for Republicans.

[6] This allows me to analyze important legislation often previously omitted, such as President Bill Clinton's attempt to reform the health-care system. Although President Clinton's proposal never experienced a floor vote (or even a committee vote), it was seriously considered – and rejected.

become laws or do not. With the winning-key-votes variable, however, it requires a little more effort. Specifically, I must employ a selection model to account for presidents' success in key votes in the endgame *given that the issue got to that point via the earlygame.* The selection model is appropriate, therefore, because it allows us to account for both processes simultaneously. The dependent variable for the selection stage is 1 if there was a key vote on the issue and 0 if not; the dependent variable for the outcome stage (as described previously) is 1 if the president's side prevailed and 0 if it did not.

A.1.2   Independent Variable
One of my argument's central tenets has been that most presidential influence requires presidential lobbying. Proposing legislation is not enough. To capture this point empirically, the president's involvement was determined through a content analysis of each bill's coverage in the relevant *CQ Almanac.* In practice, this entailed research assistants coding whether the president was "not mentioned (beyond mere signing)" (0), "clearly endorsed a position before the issue was decided in Congress" (1), or "actively lobbied in support of a particular position" (2). Research assistants agreed on presidents' involvement in the basic three categories (played no role, endorsed a position, or actively lobbied) in 93.5 percent of the double-coded cases ($n = 249$).

A.1.3   Control Variables
To isolate the relationship between presidential lobbying and congressional response (i.e., winning key votes and passing preferred legislation), the analyses in Chapters 4 and 5 account for a myriad of other related factors. These control variables focus on three basic areas: congressional predispositions, the political environment, and the particulars of each issue/bill. Let me briefly describe each.

A.1.3.1   Congressional predispositions. The first and most obvious factor affecting legislation is the predispositions of the legislature. Drawing on the pivotal-politics model, we know that each chamber's pivotal voter plays a decisive role in settling legislative debates. Because my interest is in positive presidential power – that is, presidents' ability to move laws toward the president's position – the pivotal voters are the filibuster pivot in the Senate and the median voter in the House. To standardize pivotal voters' position vis-à-vis the president, I measure pivotal voters' distance from the president in relation to the president's preferred side – pure liberal (–1) or pure conservative (+1) – using DW-NOMINATE scores, which estimate members' ideological predispositions by comparing their voting choices across an entire Congress (see Poole and Rosenthal 1997).

In addition to pivotal voters' important role in deciding what will pass, agenda-setting processes also help shape congressional outcomes (see esp. Aldrich and Rhode 2001; Cox and McCubbins 1993, 2006). As such, I control for the potential that the existence of a unified or divided government affects which bills make it to the floor for a key vote.

A.1.3.2 Political environment. After obvious congressional factors, the next contextual variables that can affect the president's fate are those related to the prevailing political environment. One that has received abundant attention is "political capital" – the confluence of circumstances that shape lawmakers' receptivity to the president and his position. Two of the more important factors underlying a president's political standing are (1) his popularity in the polls, and (2) the state of the national economy. Accordingly, presidents' political capital is measured as a factor score of presidents' yearly average presidential job approval (source: Gallup) and the nation's change in gross domestic product from the previous year (source: Bureau of Economic Analysis, U.S. Department of Commerce). To facilitate interpretation, I cut this political capital variable into thirds: low (1), medium (2), and high (3). Although I consider this a political-environment variable because the president cannot significantly shape the national economy or public opinion, this is not to say that it is unimportant for inferences about presidents' influence in Congress. Indeed, I have argued that the opposite is true; for factors the president does manipulate, political capital enhances or detracts from the effectiveness of his manipulation.

Additionally, popular and scholarly accounts emphasize the "honeymoon" period as one in which presidents' influence is greatest (see Beckmann and Godfrey 2007; Light 1999; D. Peterson et al. 2003), while others have noted the transpose: presidents' "lame duck" status renders them less influential, offsetting the benefit they would otherwise see from the experience gained during their tenure (see esp. Light 1999). I account for a president's honeymoon and lame duck status with a dummy variable for his inaugural Congress after being elected, as well as the last Congress of his second term. I also account for potential increases in presidents' effectiveness over time by controlling for each president's tenure in office, which I code as the number of Congresses the president has confronted at that point.

One more element of the political context that can affect presidents' ability to push legislation is what else is on their plate – be it scandals, financial crises, foreign affairs, or something else. The idea is that a distracted president will be less able to promote and pass his legislative agenda. To account for major exogenous events that might derail a president's legislative agenda, I include a variable, based on Lebo and Cassino's (2007) taxonomy of key events during presidents' terms, excluding those related to domestic legislation. The measure counts all such events occurring during a year, and it runs from 1 to 7, with a median of 3.

A.1.3.3 Issue specifics. The last factors likely to affect congressional processes are the issues themselves. For example, if health issues are especially important, initiatives in that domain could be more likely to reach the floor, more likely to pass. To address this potential, I include each issue area in the selection model. I also control whether a particular initiative was especially salient by monitoring its coverage (in 100s of words) in the corresponding *CQ Almanac.*

References

Aldrich, John. 1995. *Why Parties? The Origin and Transformation of Political Parties in America.* Chicago: University of Chicago Press.

Aldrich, John, and David Rohde. 2001. "The Logic of Conditional Party Government." In *Congress Reconsidered*, eds. Lawrence Dodd and Bruce Oppenheimer. Washington, DC: Congressional Quarterly Press, 269–292.

Andres, Gary, Patrick Griffin, and James Thurber. 2000. "The Contemporary Presidency: Managing White House–Congressional Relations: Observations from Inside the Process." *Presidential Studies Quarterly* 30(3): 553–563.

Arnold, R. Douglas. 1990. *The Logic of Congressional Action.* New Haven, CT: Yale University Press.

Arrow, Kenneth J. 1951. *Social Choice and Individual Values.* New York: Wiley.

Barber, James D. 1972. *The Presidential Character: Predicting Performance in the White House.* Englewood Cliffs, NJ: Prentice-Hall.

Barrett, Andrew W., and Matthew Eshbaugh-Soha. 2007. "Presidential Success on the Substance of Legislation." *Political Research Quarterly* 60(1): 100–112.

Barrett, Andrew W., and Jeffrey S. Peake. 2007. "When the President Comes to Town: Examining Local Newspaper Coverage of Domestic Presidential Travel." *American Politics Research* 35(1): 3–31.

Bartels, Larry. 2005. "Homer Gets a Tax Cut: Inequality and Public Policy in the American Mind." *Perspectives on Politics* 3(1): 15–31.

Baum, Matthew, and Samuel Kernell. 1999. "Has Cable Ended the Golden Age of Presidential Television?" *American Political Science Review* 93: 99–114.

Beckmann, Matthew N. 2008. "The President's Playbook: White House Strategies for Lobbying Congress." *The Journal of Politics* 70: 407–419.

Beckmann, Matthew N., and Joseph Godfrey. 2007. "The Policy Opportunities in Presidential Honeymoons." *Political Research Quarterly* 60(2): 250–262.

Beckmann, Matthew N., and Vimal Kumar. Forthcoming. "How Presidents Push, When Presidents Win: Locating Presidential Power in Congress." *Journal of Theoretical Politics.*

Black, Duncan. 1948. "On the Rationale of Group Decision-Making." *Journal of Political Economy* 56(1): 23–34.

Bond, Jon R., and Richard Fleisher. 1990. *The President in the Legislative Arena.* Chicago: University of Chicago Press.

Bond, Jon R., and Richard Fleisher, Eds. 2000. *Polarized Politics: Congress and the President in a Partisan Era.* Washington, DC: CQ Press.

Bond, Jon R., Richard Fleisher, and Glen Krutz. 1996. "An Overview of the Empirical Findings on Presidential–Congressional Relations." In James A. Thurber (Ed.), *Rivals for Power.* Washington, DC: CQ Press.

Brace, Paul, and Barbara Hinckley. 1992. *Follow the Leader: Opinion Polls and the Modern Presidents.* New York: Basic Books.

Brady, David W., and Craig Volden. 1998. *Revolving Gridlock: Politics and Policy from Carter to Clinton.* Boulder, CO: Westview.

Brody, Richard A. 1991. *Assessing the President: The Media, Elite Opinion, and Public Support.* Stanford, CA: Stanford University Press.

Burke, John P. 1992. *The Institutional Presidency.* Baltimore, MD: Johns Hopkins University Press.

Burns, James MacGregor. 1965. *Presidential Government: The Crucible of Leadership.* Boston: Houghton Mifflin.

Cameron, Charles. 2000. *Veto Bargaining: Presidents and the Politics of Negative Power.* New York: Cambridge University Press.

Campbell, Andrea, Gary W. Cox, and Mathew D. McCubbins. 2002. "Agenda Power in the Senate, 1877 to 1986." In *Party, Process, and Political Change in Congress: New Perspectives on the History of Congress,* eds. David Brady and Mathew McCubbins. Stanford, CA: Stanford University Press.

Canes-Wrone, Brandice. 2001. "The President's Legislative Influence from Public Appeals." *American Journal of Political Science* 45(2): 313–329.

Canes-Wrone, Brandice. 2005. *Who Leads Whom? Presidents, Policy Making and the American Public.* Chicago: University of Chicago Press.

Canes-Wrone, Brandice, and Scott de Marchi. 2002. "Presidential Approval and Legislative Success." *The Journal of Politics* 64: 491–509.

Canes-Wrone, Brandice, William Howell, and David E. Lewis. 2008. "Toward a Broader Understanding of Presidential Power: A Reevaluation of the Two Presidencies Thesis." *The Journal of Politics* 70(1): 1–16.

Cannon, Lou. 2000. *President Reagan: The Role of a Lifetime.* New York: Public Affairs.

Carter, Jimmy. 1995. *Keeping Faith.* Little Rock: University of Arkansas.

Cohen, Jeffrey E. 1997. *Presidential Responsiveness and Public Policymaking: The Publics and the Policies That Presidents Choose.* Ann Arbor: University of Michigan Press.

Cohen, Jeffrey E. 2008. *The Presidency in the Era of 24-Hour News.* Princeton, NJ: Princeton University Press.

Cohen, Richard E. 1992. *Washington at Work: Back Rooms and Clean Air.* New York: Macmillan.

Collier, Kenneth E. 1997. *Between the Branches: The White House Office of Legislative Affairs.* Pittsburgh, PA: University of Pittsburgh Press.

Conley, Patricia Heidotting. 2001. *Presidential Mandates: How Elections Shape the National Agenda.* Chicago: University of Chicago Press.

Conley, Richard S. 2002. *The Presidency, Congress, and Divided Government: A Post-War Assessment.* College Station: Texas A&M University Press.

Conley, Richard S., and Richard M. Yon. 2007. "The 'Hidden Hand' and White House Roll-Call Predictions: Legislative Liaison in the Eisenhower White House, 83d–84th Congresses." *Presidential Studies Quarterly* 37(2): 291–312.

Corwin, Edward S. 1957. *The President: Office and Powers, 1787–1957: History and Analysis of Practice and Opinion.* New York: New York University Press.

Covington, Cary R. 1986. "Congressional Support for the President: View from the Kennedy–Johnson White House." *The Journal of Politics* 48: 717–728.

Covington, Cary R. 1987. "Staying Private: Gaining Congressional Support for Unpublicized Presidential Preferences on Roll Call Votes." *The Journal of Politics* 49(3): 737–755.

Covington, Cary R. 1988. "Building Presidential Coalitions among Cross Pressured Members of Congress." *Western Politics Quarterly* 41(1): 47–62.

Covington, Cary R., Mark J. Wrighton, and Rhonda Kinney. 1995. "A 'Presidency-Augmented' Model of Presidential Success on House Roll Call Votes." *American Journal of Political Science* 39(4): 1001–1024.

Cox, Gary W., and Jonathan N. Katz. 2007. "Gerrymandering Roll-Calls in Congress, 1879–2000." *American Journal of Political Science* 51(1): 108–119.

Cox, Gary W., and Mathew D. McCubbins. 1993. *Legislative Leviathan: Party Government in the House.* Berkeley: University of California Press.

Cox, Gary W., and Mathew D. McCubbins. 2005. *Setting the Agenda: Responsible Party Government in the U.S. House of Representatives.* New York: Cambridge University Press.

Cronin, Thomas E. 1970. "Everybody Believes in Democracy until He Gets to the White House...': An Examination of White House-Departmental Relations." *Law and Contemporary Problems* 35(3): 573–625.

Dahl, Robert A. 1956. *A Preface to Democratic Theory.* Chicago: University of Chicago Press.

Dahl, Robert A. 1990. "Myth of the Presidential Mandate." *Political Science Quarterly* 105(3): 355–372.

Dewar, Helen."Reagan Woos Budget Waverers; Democrats Bewail Favors Game." *The Washington Post.* 2 May 1981, 5(A).

Dickinson, Matthew J. 1997. *Bitter Harvest: FDR, Presidential Power, and the Growth of the Presidential Branch.* New York: Cambridge University Press.

Dickinson, Matthew J. 2008. "The Politics of Persuasion: A Bargaining Model of Presidential Power." In *Presidential Leadership: The Vortex of Power,* eds. Bert Rockman and Richard Waterman. New York: Oxford University Press.

Downs, Anthony. 1957. *An Economic Theory of Democracy.* New York: Harper.

Drew, Elizabeth. 1996. *Showdown: The Struggle between the Gingrich Congress and the Clinton White House.* New York: Touchstone.

Edwards, George C., III. 1983. *The Public Presidency: The Pursuit of Popular Support.* New Haven, CT: Yale University Press.

Edwards, George C., III. 1989. *At the Margins: Presidential Leadership of Congress.* New Haven, CT: Yale University Press.

Edwards, George C., III. 2003. *On Deaf Ears: The Limits of the Bully Pulpit.* New Haven, CT: Yale University Press.

Edwards, George C., III, and Andrew Barrett. 2000. "Presidential Agenda-Setting in Congress." In *Polarized Politics: Congress and the President in a Partisan Era,* eds. Jon Bond and Richard Fleisher. Washington, DC: Congressional Quarterly Press, 109–133.

Edwards III, George C., Andrew Barrett, and Jeffrey Peake. 1997. "The Legislative Impact of Divided Government." *American Journal of Political Science* 41(2): 545–563.

Edwards, George C., III, and B. Dan Wood. 1999. "Who Influences Whom? The President and the Public Agenda." *American Political Science Review* 93(2): 327–344.

Evans, C. Lawrence. 1991. *Leadership in Committee: A Comparative Analysis of Leadership Behavior in the U.S. Senate.* Ann Arbor: University of Michigan Press.

Fenno, Richard. 1978. *Home Style: House Members in their Districts.* New York: Little, Brown.

Fett, Patrick. 1994. "Presidential Legislative Priorities and Legislators' Voting Decisions: An Exploratory Analysis." *Journal of Politics* 56(2): 502–512.

Fiorina, Morris P. 1974. *Representatives, Roll Calls, and Constituencies*. Lexington, MA: Lexington Books.

Fiorina, Morris P. 1981. *Retrospective Voting in American National Elections*. New Haven, CT: Yale University Press.

Fleisher, Richard, and Jon R. Bond. 2000. "Partisanship and the President's Quest for Votes on the Floor of Congress." In *Polarized Politics: Congress and the President in a Partisan Era*, eds. Jon Bond and Richard Fleisher. Washington, DC: Congressional Quarterly Press, 154–185.

Fortier, John C., and Norman J. Ornstein. 2003. "President Bush: Legislative Strategist." In *The George W. Bush Presidency: An Early Assessment*, ed. Fred I. Greenstein. Baltimore, MD: Johns Hopkins University Press.

Gallup, George H. 2002. *The Gallup Poll 2001*. New York: Scholarly Resources, Inc.

Gans, Herbert J. 1979. *Deciding What's News: A Study of CBS Evening News, NBC Nightly News, Newsweek and Time*. New York: Vintage Books.

Gilmour, John B. 2002. "Institutional and Individual Influences on the President's Veto." *Journal of Politics* 64(1): 198–218.

Green, William H. 2007. *Econometric Analysis*, 6th ed. New York: Prentice Hall.

Greenstein, Fred I. 1982. *The Hidden-Hand President: Eisenhower as Leader*. New York: Basic Books.

Grofman, Bernard. 2004. "Downs and Two-Party Convergence". *Annual Review of Political Science* 7: 25–46.

Groseclose, Timothy, and James M. Snyder, Jr. 1996. "Buying Supermajorities." *American Political Science Review* 90(2): 303–315.

Grossback, Lawrence J., David A. M. Peterson, and James A. Stimson. 2005. "Comparing Competing Theories on the Causes of Mandate Perceptions." *American Journal of Political Science* 49: 406–419.

Grossman, Michael B., and Martha Joynt Kumar. 1981. *Portraying the President*. Baltimore, MD: Johns Hopkins University Press.

Hacker, Jacob S., and Paul Pierson. 2006. *Off Center: The Republican Revolution and the Erosion of American Democracy*. New Haven, CT: Yale University Press.

Hager, Gregory, and Terry Sullivan. 1994. "President-Centered and Presidency-Centered Explanations of Presidential Public Activity." *American Journal of Political Science* 38: 1079–1103.

Hall, Richard L. 1996. *Participation in Congress*. New Haven, CT: Yale University Press.

Hall, Richard L., and Matthew N. Beckmann. 2004. The Legislative Politics of Protectionism. Working Paper. University of Michigan.

Hall, Richard L., and Kristina Miler. 2008. "What Happens After the Alarm? Interest Group Subsidies to Legislative Overseers." *Journal of Politics* 70(4): 1–16.

Hightower, Jim. 2007. *There's Nothing in the Middle of the Road but Yellow Stripes and Dead Armadillos.* New York: HarperCollins.

Howell, William. 2003. *Power without Persuasion.* Princeton, NJ: Princeton University Press.

Hughes, Emmet John. 1963. *The Ordeal of Power: A Political Memoir of the Eisenhower Years.* New York: Athenaeum.

Iyengar, Shanto, and Donald Kinder. 1987. *News that Matters.* Chicago: University of Chicago Press.

Jacobson, Gary C. 2000. *The Politics of Congressional Elections.* 5th ed. New York: Longman.

Jacobson, Gary C. 2004. *A Divider, Not a Uniter: George W. Bush and the American People.* New York: Longman.

Johnson, Lyndon B. 1971. *The Vantage Point.* New York: Holt Rinehart and Winston.

Jones, Charles O. 1994. *The Presidency in a Separated System.* Washington, DC: Brookings Institution press.

Kearns Goodwin, Doris. 1991. *Lyndon Johnson and the American Dream.* New York: St. Martin's Press.

Kellerman, Barbara. 1984. *The Political Presidency.* New York: Oxford University Press.

Kernell, Samuel. 1993. *Going Public: New Strategies of Presidential Leadership.* Washington, DC: Congressional Quarterly Press.

Kiewiet, D. Roderick, and Mathew D. McCubbins. 1988. "Presidential Influence on Congressional Appropriations Decisions." *American Journal of Political Science* 32: 713–736.

Kiewiet, D. Roderick, and Mathew D. McCubbins. 1991. *The Logic of Delegation.* Chicago: University of Chicago Press.

King, Anthony. 1983. *Both Ends of the Avenue: The Presidency, the Executive Branch, and Congress in the 1980s.* Washington, DC: American Enterprise Institute.

King, David C., and Richard Zeckhauser. 2003. Congressional Vote Options. *Legislative Studies Quarterly* 28(3): 387–411.

Kingdon, John W. 1989. *Congressmen's Voting Decisions.* 3rd ed. Ann Arbor: University of Michigan Press.

Kingdon, John W. 1995. *Agendas, Alternatives, and Public Policies,* 2nd ed. New York: Addison-Wesley Education Publishers, Inc.

Kotz, Nick. 2005. *Judgment Days: Lyndon Baines Johnson, Martin Luther King Jr., and the Laws that Changed America.* New York: Mariner Books.

Kramer, Gerald. 1983. "The Ecological Fallacy Revisited: Aggregate versus Individual-Level Findings on Economics and Elections, and Sociotropic Voting." *American Political Science Review* 77: 92–111.

Krehbiel, Keith. 1991. *Information and Legislative Organization.* Ann Arbor: University of Michigan Press.

Krehbiel, Keith. 1998. *Pivotal Politics: A Theory of U.S. Lawmaking*. Chicago: University of Chicago Press.

Krugman, Paul. 2001. "Reckoning; Guns and Bitterness" [op-ed]. *The New York Times*, Feb. 4.

Kumar, Martha J. 2007. *Managing the President's Message: The White House Coummunications Operation*. Baltimore, MD: Johns Hopkins University Press.

Lebo, Matthew J., and Daniel Cassino. 2007. "The Aggregated Consequences of Motivated Reasoning and the Dynamics of Partisan Presidential Approval." *Political Psychology* 28(6): 719–746.

Lewis, David E., and James M. Strinc. 1996. "What Time Is It? The Use of Power in Four Different Types of Presidential Time." *Journal of Politics* 58(3): 682–706.

Lieberman, Robert C. 2000. "Political Time and Policy Coalitions." In *Presidential Power: Forging the Presidency for the 21st Century*, eds. Robert Shapiro, Martha Joynt Kumar, and Larry Jacobs. New York: Columbia University Press.

Light, Paul C. 1999. *The President's Agenda: Domestic Policy Choice from Kennedy to Clinton*. 3rd ed. Baltimore, MD: Johns Hopkins University Press.

Lockerbie, Brad, Stephen Borrelli, and Scott Hedger. 1998. "An Integrative Approach to Modeling Presidential Success in Congress." *Political Research Quarterly* 51(1): 155–172.

Long, J. Scott. 1997. *Regression Models for Categorical and Limited Dependent Variables*. Vol. 7. Newbury Park, CA: Sage.

Lott, Trent. 2005. *Herding Cats: A Life in Politics*. New York: HarperCollins.

Mann, Robert T. 1992. *Legacy to Power: Senator Russell Long of Louisiana*. New York: Universal Sales & Marketing.

Mayer, Kenneth R. 2001. *With the Stroke of a Pen: Executive Orders and Presidential Power*. Princeton, NJ: Princeton University Press.

Mayhew, David R. 1974. *Congress: The Electoral Connection*. New Haven, CT: Yale University Press.

Mayhew, David R. 2005. *Divided We Govern: Party Control, Lawmaking, and Investigations, 1946–2002*. New Haven, CT: Yale University Press.

McKelvey, Richard D. 1976. "Intransitivities in Multidimensional Voting Models and Some Implications for Agenda Control." *Journal of Economic Theory* 12(3): 472–482.

Miller Center of Public Affairs. 2000. "The Presidential Recordings Project: 'The Lyndon Johnson Treatment.'" Miller Center Report. Charlottesville: Miller Center of Public Affairs, University of Virginia, Vol. 16, No. 1, 25–28.

Mitchell, Allison. 2000. "The 43rd President: The President-Elect; President-Elect Courts Congress and Urges Tax Cut." *The New York Times*, Dec. 19, A1.

Moe, Terry M. 1984. "The New Economics of Organization." *American Journal of Political Science* 28(4): 739–777.

Moe, Terry M. 1993. "Presidents, Institutions, and Theory." In *Researching the Presidency: Vital Questions, New Approaches*, eds. George C. Edwards III, John H. Kessel, and Bert A. Rockman. Pittsburgh, PA: University of Pittsburgh Press.

Moe, Terry, and William G. Howell. 1999. "The Presidential Power of Unilateral Action." *Journal of Law, Economics and Organizations* 15(1): 132–179.

Morris, Dick. 1998. *Behind the Oval Office: Getting Reelected against All Odds.* New York: Renaissance Books.

Neustadt, Richard. 1990[1960]. *Presidential Power and the Modern Presidents.* New York: Free Press.

Page, Benjamin I., and Robert Y. Shapiro. 1992. *The Rational Public: Fifty Years of Trends in Americans' Policy Preferences.* Chicago: University of Chicago Press.

Patterson, Samuel H. 2000. *The White House Staff: Inside the West Wing and Beyond.* Washington, DC: Brookings Institution Press.

Peterson, David A. M., Lawrence J. Grossback, James A. Stimson, and Amy Gangl. 2003. "Congressional Response to Mandate Elections." *American Journal of Political Science* 47: 411–426.

Peterson, Mark A. 1990. *Legislating Together: The White House and Capitol Hill from Eisenhower to Reagan.* Cambridge: Harvard University Press.

Pitkin, Hannah F. 1967. *The Concept of Representation.* Berkeley: University of California Press.

Ponder, Daniel E. 2000. *Good Advice: Information and Policy Making in the White House.* College Station: Texas A&M University Press.

Poole, Keith T., and Howard Rosenthal. 1997. *Congress: A Political-Economic History of Roll Call Voting.* New York: Oxford University Press.

Pritchard, Anita. 1983. "Presidents Do Influence Voting in the US Congress: New Definitions and Measurements." *Legislative Studies Quarterly* 8(4): 691–711.

Rabinowitz, George, and Stuart Elaine Macdonald. 1989. "A Directional Theory of Issue Voting." *American Political Science Review* 83: 93–121.

Rivers, Douglas, and Nancy Rose. 1985. "Passing a President's Program: Public Opinion and Presidential Influence in Congress." *American Journal of Political Science* 29: 183–196.

Rohde, David W. 1991. *Parties and Leaders in the Postreform House.* Chicago: University of Chicago Press.

Romer, Thomas, and Howard Rosenthal. 1978. "Political Resource Allocation: Controlled Agendas and the Status Quo." *Public Choice* 33(4): 27–43.

Roosevelt, Theodore. 1985[1913]. *Theodore Roosevelt: An Autobiography.* New York: Da Capo Press.

Rossiter, Clinton. 1956. *The American Presidency.* New York: New American Library of World Literature.

Rudalevige, Andrew. 2002. *Managing the President's Program: Presidential Leadership and Legislative Policy Formation.* Princeton, NJ: Princeton University Press.

Schlesinger, Arthur M. 1973. *The Imperial Presidency.* New York: Houghton Mifflin.

Shull, Steven A., and James M. Vanderleeuw. 1987. "What do Key Votes Measure?" *Legislative Studies Quarterly* 12(4): 573–582.

Sigelman, Lee, and Carol K. Sigelman. 1981. "Presidential Leadership of Public Opinion: From 'Benevolent Leader' to Kiss of Death'?" *Experimental Study of Politics* 7(3): 1–22.

Sinclair, Barbara. 1983. *Majority Leadership in the U.S. House.* Baltimore, MD: Johns Hopkins University Press.

Sinclair, Barbara. 1993. "Studying Presidential Leadership." In *Researching the Presidency,* eds. George C. Edwards, John H. Kessel, and Bert A. Rockman. Pittsburgh, PA: University of Pittsburgh Press, 387–412.

Sinclair, Barbara. 1995. *Legislators, Leaders, and Lawmaking: The U.S. House of Representatives in the Postreform Era.* Baltimore, MD: Johns Hopkins University Press.

Sinclair, Barbara. 2006. *Party Wars: Polarization and the Politics of National Policymaking.* Norman, OK: University of Oklahoma Press.

Skowronek, Stephen. 1993. *The Politics Presidents Make: Leadership from John Adams to Bill Clinton.* Cambridge, MA: Harvard University Press.

Smith, Steven S. 1989. *Call to Order: Floor Politics in the House and Senate.* Washington, DC: Brookings Institution Press.

Smith, Steven S. 2007. *Party Influence in Congress.* New York: Cambridge University Press.

Snyder, James M., Jr. 1991. "On Buying Legislatures." *Economics and Politics* 3(2): 93–109.

Sperlich, Peter. 1975. "Bargaining and Overload." In *Perspectives on the Presidency,* ed. Aaron B. Wildavsky. Boston: Little, Brown.

Stephanopoulos, George. 1999. *All Too Human: A Political Education.* New York: Back Bay.

Stevenson, Richard W. 2001. "Fed Cuts Key Rate by Half a Point, Citing Slowdown." *The New York Times,* Feb. 1.

Sullivan, Terry. 1987. "Presidential Leadership in Congress: Securing Commitments." In *Congress: Structure and Policy,* eds. Mathew McCubbins and Terry Sullivan. Cambridge, UK: Cambridge University Press.

Sullivan, Terry. 1988. "Headcounts, Expectations, and Presidential Coalitions in Congress." *American Journal of Political Science* 32(3): 567–589.

Sullivan, Terry. 1990. "Explaining Why Presidents Count: Signaling and Information." *Journal of Politics* 52(3): 939–962.

Sullivan, Terry. 1991. "Bargaining with the President: A Simple Game and New Evidence." *American Political Science Review* 84(4): 1167–1195.

Taft, William Howard. 1975[1916]. *Our Chief Magistrate*. South Hackensack, NJ: Rothman Reprints.

Thurber, James. 2006. *Rivals for Power: Presidential–Congressional Relations*, 3rd ed. New York: Rowman & Littlefield Publishers, Inc.

Van Houweling, Robert P. 2003. *Legislators' Personal Policy Preferences and Partisan Legislative Organization*. Dissertation. Harvard University.

Walcott, Charles E., and Karen M. Hult. 1995. *Governing the White House: From Hoover to LBJ*. Lawrence: University of Kansas Press.

Warshaw, Shirley Anne. 1997. *The Domestic Presidency: Policy Making in the White House*. Boston: Allyn and Bacon.

Wattenberg, Martin P. 1991. *The Rise of Candidate-Centered Politics: Presidential Elections of the 1980s*. Cambridge, MA: Harvard University Press.

Wattenberg, Martin P. 1998. *The Decline of American Political Parties*. 6th ed. Cambridge, MA: Harvard University Press.

Wattenberg, Martin P. 2004. "Elections: Tax Cut versus Lockbox: Did the Voters Grasp the Tradeoff in 2000?" *Presidential Studies Quarterly* 34(4): 838–848.

Wawro, Gregory. 2001. *Legislative Entrepreneurship in the U.S. House of Representatives*. Ann Arbor: University of Michigan Press.

Wildavsky, Aaron. 1969. "The Two Presidencies." In *The Presidency*. Aaron Wildavsky, Ed. Boston: Little, Brown.

Wilson, Woodrow, *Congressional Government*. New York, Houghton Mifflin, 1885.

Wilson, Woodrow. 1981. *Congressional Government: A Study in American Politics*. Baltimore, MD: Johns Hopkins University Press.

Wolfinger, Raymond E. 1985. "Dealignment, Realignment, and Mandates in the 1984 Election." In *The American Elections of 1984*, ed. Austin Ranney. Washington, DC: American Enterprise Institute and Duke University Press.

Woolley, John T., and Gerhard Peters. *The American Presidency Project* [online]. Santa Barbara, CA: University of California (hosted), Gerhard Peters (database). Available at www.presidency.ucsb.edu.

Zaller, John R. 1992. *The Nature and Origins of Mass Opinion*. New York: Cambridge University Press.

Index

agenda-centered strategy, of presidents,
   21–22
  ally mobilization in, 54–55
  consequences of, 58–62
  lobbying and, 21–22, 50–62, 96
  logic of, 53–62
  opponent deterrence in, 55–58
  "pivotal voters" and, 34, 57
  for tax cut policy, for Bush, G. W.,
   81–83
  in tax cut strategy of Bush, G. W., 96
agenda-setting, by presidents, 17–19, 20
  earlygame strategy with, 50–62
  lobbying and, 20, 50–62
  negative agenda control and, 41–42
  policy making and, 35–37, 40
  as politically compromising, 57–58
  positive agenda control and, 42, 44
  presidential power through, 17–20
  for proposals, 36–37
Armey, Dick, 73

Baker, Howard, 39
Baker, James, 51
Barrett, Andrew, 19, 36
Baucus, Max, 103
Berlin Wall, fall of, 13
Black, Duncan, 31
Bond, Jon, 36, 53, 167
Bonier, David, 75
Brady, Henry, 7
Breaux, John, 78
Brown v. Board of Education of Topeka, 13
budget reconciliation process, 77
"bully pulpit," presidency as, 18
Burns, James MacGregor, 14–15

Bush, George H. W., 16–17
Bush, George W., 25, 28, 111 *See also* tax
  cuts, strategy of Bush, G. W.
  lobbying success of, 134–135, 145
  perception of Congress, 3
  political pragmatism of, 155
  presidential leadership of, 153–154
  Social Security reform campaign of,
   153, 154
  tax cut policy under, strategy for,
   68–105
  on vote counting, 31
  vote-centered strategy of, 47
Byrd, Robert, 39

Caddell, Patrick, 12
Calio, Nick, 158
Cannon, Lou, 160
Carter, Jimmy, 12
  Congressional battles of, 6, 55–59
  "discredited" presidency of, 10
  ideological support in Congress
   for, 8
  key votes for, perceived success with,
   106–108
  legislative proposals under, negative
   success from involvement, 135
  lobbying success of, 135, 146, 148
  political pragmatism of, 160
  problem prioritization for, 152
  vote-centered strategy of, 47
Celler, Emanuel, 129
Civil Rights Act of 1964, 129
Clinton, Bill, 106
  on budget fights with Congress, 28
  endgame strategy for, 51

Made in the USA
Lexington, KY
24 January 2015